D0027963

DEPRAVED
and
INSULTING
ENGLISH

DEPRAVED
and
INSULTING
ENGLISH

PETER NOVOBATZKY

and

AMMON SHEA

A Harvest Original • Harcourt, Inc.
San Diego   New York   London

Copyright © 2001, 1999 by Peter Novobatzky and Ammon Shea

All rights reserved. No part of this publication may be reproduced
or transmitted in any form or by any means, electronic or mechanical,
including photocopy, recording, or any information storage and retrieval
system, without permission in writing from the publisher.

Requests for permission to make copies of any part of the work should be
mailed to the following address: Permissions Department, Harcourt, Inc.,
6277 Sea Harbor Drive, Orlando, Florida 32887-6777.

www.HarcourtBooks.com

Library of Congress Cataloging-in-Publication Data
Novobatzky, Peter.
Depraved and insulting English/
Peter Novobatzky and Ammon Shea.—1st ed.
p.   cm.—(Harvest book)
ISBN 0-15-601149-2
1. English language—Obscene words—Dictionaries.
2. English language—Obsolete words—Dictionaries.
3. English language—Slang—Dictionaries.   4. Invective—Dictionaries.
5. Vocabulary.   I. Shea, Ammon.   II. Title.
PE3721 .N677 2002
427'.09—dc21   2002000479

Text set in Sabon
Display set in Bostonia and Basketcase
Designed by Cathy Riggs

Printed in the United States of America

First edition

H

For our parents

Introduction

Amidst the grand panoply that is the English language, largest on this Earth, tongue of Shakespeare, Byron, and Melville, there are a puzzling number of words that mean "to spray with shit."

Truth to tell, English teems with obscure—and hilarious—depraved and insulting words, which most educated people have never heard of. A multitude of sexual and scatological terms, like *bescumber,* and *pizzle;* a legion of terms for offensive or pathetic people, such as *muscod, nullimitus,* and *raddled.*

This fact led to our first book, *Depraved English,* which focused on the perverse and unseemly side of our lexicon, and eventually also to *Insulting English,* which tried to provide a word for every type of insult-worthy person. *Depraved and Insulting English* represents a fusion of the two earlier books; our editors feeling (and we agreeing) that their contents are compatible enough to co-exist between the covers of the same volume.

A lexicon such as this is not meant to be read straight through. Better to dip into it at random. Even a casual glance will reveal that some of the entries are lascivious, some revolting, and others derogatory. A few are all of these things. Many of the featured words are quite old, others are relatively new. Some were common in another time or place, while others have never been particularly popular. There are words (*feague* comes to mind) for objects, practices, and states of being one never knew existed, side by side with words like *frottage*, which describe things one probably knew existed but never knew there was a word for. A choice few, such as *groak* and *urinous*, are readily applicable in everyday life.

Most if not all of the words listed in *Depraved and Insulting English* are likely to be as new to the reader as they were to us when we first came across them in our research. But rest assured that they are all real English words, culled from a wide variety of sources. Current and out-of-print dictionaries, cyclopedias, specialty lexicons, word books, and medical dictionaries were among the works consulted. For a full list, see the bibliography at the end of the book.

The authors take full responsibility for the sentences illustrating the words in action. These, along with the little informative paragraphs accompanying the entries—as well as the odd limerick—are our creations. Writing them enabled us to vent a lot of spleen we had built up over the years; so much so that on several occasions we actually found ourselves running low on spleen.

Obviously, the average reader cannot be expected to commit to memory a large proportion of the words in this book. Still, we hope that at least a few terms will resonate enough to be recalled later. After all, a good vocabulary is not only a sign of education and intelligence; knowing the proper word for something sharpens the powers of perception. For example, once a word like *shotclog* becomes lodged in your brain, you will begin for the first time to see *shotclogs* popping up everywhere. Your eyes will have been opened up to an entire sub-type of humanity that had previously escaped notice.

While *Depraved and Insulting English* aspires to be a useful resource for verbal aggressors, in the end its main concern is simply to help readers describe the world and the people in it with succinct and precise terminology. We think it will amaze and amuse, and give people a taste of what an inexhaustible and bizarre language English really is. And we dare to hope that a few of our readers will come to use at least a handful of these verbal gems in their daily lives—perhaps on their friends and loved ones.

A Note on the Entries

All the entries in *Depraved and Insulting English* are, to the best of our knowledge and according to painstaking research, actual, legitimate English words. The pronunciation guides were designed with American accents in mind. Where the sources list various pronunciations, we have selected what we feel to be the best one. Similarly, where the sources disagree as to the spelling or definition of a particular word, or where different versions exist, we have exercised whatever common sense and lexicographical judgment has been granted us by the fates.

DEPRAVED
and
INSULTING
ENGLISH

ablutophobic /*ab LOOT o FO bik*/ adj • Pathologically afraid of bathing.

[Latin *ablutio* a washing + Greek *phobos* fear]

"To punish him for committing the unnatural act with the chalkboard eraser, Mrs. Schneider forced Henry to sit every day next to the **ablutophobic** girl, the one with the thick pigtails and the faint but unmistakable odor of old sausage about her."   (*compare* **odorivector, stinkard**)

aboiement /*ah bwah MAHN*/ n • Involuntary blurting of animal noises, such as barking.

"The personal ad read simply, 'Handsome SWM, financially secure, seeks SWF for romance, possibly more. **Aboiement** a +,' but Marjorie knew immediately that she had stumbled upon her perfect mate."

(*compare* **desticate, fream**)

abydocomist /*ab ee do CO mist*/ n • A liar who boasts of his or her falsehood.

"There were lots of **abydocomists** working the phones at the underground telemarketing firm, but none could top Neville, who would cheerfully swindle a widowed grandmother out of her annuity fund and then climb atop his desk and trumpet, 'I am the king of the lying worms!'"

(*compare* **fissilingual**)

acalculiac /ay kal KOOL ee ak/ n • Someone who cannot count or do simple math.

"Mortimer could remember exactly when he became disgusted with being a high school math teacher. It was the day he met with the principal to discuss the **acalculiacs** in his freshman class, and the old bureaucrat kept insisting: *'Lower the bar, Mort! Lower the bar!'* "

(*compare* **agrammaticist**)

achilous /uh KAI lus/ adj • Having no lips.

One of many words scattered throughout this book that are useful for describing common turnoffs.

"Wanda was a wonderful lady, but no matter what her attributes, J.B. could never bring himself to kiss an **achilous** woman." (*compare* **chichiface**)

acokoinonia /uh ko koy NO nee uh/ n • Sex without passion.

Otherwise known as "the doldrums." Or, for some unlucky marrieds, "as good as it gets." (*compare* **artamesia**)

acrocephalic /AK ro sef AL ik/ adj • Having a pointed skull.

With a bit of figurative license, this word may be extended to cover anything that might be called "pinheaded," which gives it a very wide range indeed. For example, if you wish to tell someone that his idea is harebrained, tell him it is "**acrocephalic,** plain and simple."

"Rabbi Abramson was a devout and patient man, but the carnival sideshow wedding frustrated even him: after all, how *do* you put a yarmulke on an **acrocephalic** Jew?"

acrotophiliac /uh CRO toe FEEL ee ak/ n • A person who is sexually attracted to the stumps of amputees.

acokoinonia

One of the first words in the book, and already the authors are making fun of the infirm. It doesn't seem quite fair; after all, an amputee needs love as much as the next person. To help make it up to our lesser-limbed friends, we have decided to throw them a bone, in the form of a list detailing the correct word for every different type of person strangely and powerfully aroused by the absence of an appendage:

acrotomophiliac—One who enjoys fantasizing that his or her sexual partner is an amputee.

ameliotist—A person who is sexually attracted to an amputee as a whole, not just to his or her stump.

apotemnophiliac—One who fantasizes about being an amputee; one who schemes to amputate some part of his or her body in order to gain sexual pleasure.

monopediomaniac—Someone with a sexual attraction or psychological dependence on a one-legged person.

(*compare* **dysmorphophiliac**)

adipocere /*AD ip ose eer*/ n • A fatty, waxlike material that human and animal tissues sometimes convert into when corpses decompose underwater, and which may preserve physical features for long periods.

It may not be very funny, but **adipocere** is one of the more bizarre and ghoulish words in the language.

"Freddie Barbarossa, the cemetery king, started out at the bottom, shovel in hand and **adipocere** on his shoes."

(*compare* **engrease, gobbets**)

adulterine /*ad ULT er een*/ n • A person born of an adulterous union.

The distinction between an **adulterine** and a *bastard* is that a bastard is simply the offspring of unwed parents, while an **adulterine** is the issue of an **adulterous** union; that is, one involving folks who are married, just not to each other. Both terms derived much of their original sting from conventional attitudes, grounded in religion, toward marriage and sin. *Bastard,* however, has triumphed by evolving into a broader definition. Nowadays, calling someone a *bastard* does not necessarily mean that the person was born out of wedlock, just that he or she is mean and despicable. But while *bastard* is now a commonly used insult, **adulterine** remains stuck in its original, specific meaning, and is not often used.

(*compare* **gandermooner, uzzard, wetewold**)

aerocolpos /*air o KOLE pose*/ n • Vaginal flatulence; air or gas trapped in the vagina.

[Greek *aer* air + *kolpos* bosom or fold]

Yes, there exists a technical term for this unmentionable occurrence. So why doesn't anyone know what to properly call it? Other unappealing bodily functions are known by their official names; why does **aerocolpos** have to go by *quiff* (meaning, literally, "puff of air")? Could it be that this concept still elicits some feelings of queasiness or embarrassment with certain people? Remember, gentle reader: **aerocolpos** is as natural as breathing. Just because it often occurs during sex doesn't mean it is something to be ashamed of. (However, this does not mean that the authors cannot poke fun at it. . . .)

(*compare **eproctolagniac***)

agastopia /*ag uh STOPE ee uh*/ n • The admiration of a part of someone's body.

Everyone occasionally comes under the spell of **agastopia**; it is a proven fact that people who frequently experience it are far more likely to fall down open manholes than the population as a whole. Those who are prone to the condition but do not wish to advertise it may purchase a serviceable pair of dark sunglasses from their local five-and-dime store. (*compare **apodyopsis, gynopiper***)

agelast /*AJ uh last*/ n • A person who never laughs.

"Much to the dismay of Baffo, the drugstore-robbing clown, the sentencing judge was a stern **agelast**."

(*compare **cachinnator***)

ageustia /*ay GOOSE tee uh*/ n • Absence of a sense of taste; complete or partial loss of the sense of taste.

[*a* (neg.) + Greek *geusis* taste]

A metaphorical gem, and a useful code word to share with a friend. Symptoms of this actual medical condition include a tolerance for dubious foods, and the wearing of stripes with plaid.

"Either Janice's new in-laws possessed a highly evolved sense of humor, or they suffered from severe **ageustia.** How else to explain their wedding present, a neon cuckoo clock that blurted the theme songs from seventies sitcoms every quarter hour?" (*compare bedizen*)

agitatrix /*aj ih TAY trix*/ n • A female agitator; a woman who agitates.

Men can recognize the dreaded **agitatrix** by these telltale utterances: "Does this dress make me look fat?" "Do you think she's cute?" "Why don't you tell me you love me?" and the ever-popular "You're not allowed to fart in bed."
(*compare baratress*)

agrammaticist /*ay gram AT iss ist*/ n • One suffering from *agrammaticism*: the inability to form sentences.

"Nathan was a lifelong **agrammaticist,** but was able to put this shortcoming to good use in his chosen career: politics. Speaking entirely in disconnected sound bites, he truly was a candidate for the twenty-first century."
(*compare acalculiac*)

agrexophrenia /*uh GREX o FREE nee uh*/ n • Inability to perform sexually due to a fear of being overheard.

"Raising a large family in a quaint little Irish cottage, **agrexophrenia** was a continual problem for Mr. and Mrs. McDougal, as the clan usually slept four to a bed."
(*compare atolmia*)

aidle /*AY dl*/ v • "To earn one's bread indifferently well." (Charles Mackay's *Lost Beauties of the English Language,* 1874)

"**Aidling** away the months selling greeting cards door-to-door, Michelle didn't care if she sold two, twelve, or none at all. She did enjoy taking three-hour lunches, however, and could often be seen sitting in a quiet and shady corner of the park catching up on her reading."

*(compare **eyeservant, ploiter**)*

alacuoth /al uh KOO oth/ n • Involuntary defecation during sex.

Befouling oneself is difficult to cope with in the best of circumstances—how much more so with such unfortunate timing.

No doubt many readers will immediately cast **alacuoth** onto that dung heap of the mind where one chucks all the unpleasant things one would rather forget. But while it may be one of those words of which it is happiest to remain ignorant, it demands inclusion in any unflinching discussion of the descriptive capacities of the English language.

"Milo knew what he was looking for in a woman, and when he finally found one who didn't seem to mind his chronic **alacuoth**, he slapped a ring on her finger in two whisks of a lamb's tail."   *(compare **dyspareunia, sterky**)*

algolagnia /al go LAG nee uh/ n • The garnering of sexual thrills by inflicting or suffering pain.

"Biff's closet **algolagnia** compelled him to partake in contact sports such as tackle football and rugby, where he quickly earned a reputation as both a glutton for punishment and a sadistic bastard."   *(compare **mastigophoric**)*

allochezia /al o KEE zee uh/ n • Defecation from somewhere other than the anus. Also, defecation of something other than feces.

"Nick was suspicious of doctors as a rule, but when his **allochezia** failed to clear up by itself he decided to schedule an appointment." *(compare **copremesis, lientery**)*

allorgasmia */al or GAZ mee uh/* n • Fantasizing about someone other than one's partner during sex.

Allorgasmia is not usually something one openly discusses with one's sexual partner. But it is fairly common. What's more, the spice it brings to the bedroom probably saves more relationships than all the marital therapists west of the Missippippi. So, the next time **allorgasmia** causes the supermarket checkout girl or delivery boy to make a guest appearance in your bed—er, *head*—try not to feel too guilty about it. *(compare **anagapesis**)*

alothen */AL o then/* v • To grow disgusting.

From people to cultural phenomena to leftover tuna casserole, there are so many potential uses for the word **alothen** that the reader is encouraged to let his or her imagination run wild. *(compare **turdefy**)*

amastia */ay MAST ee uh/* n • Lack of breasts.

"He was a born con man who got his start in crime as a teenager, hustling a vile-tasting potion which he claimed could cure **amastia**." *(compare **micromastia**)*

amatorculist */am at or COOL ist/* n • A pitiful or insignificant lover.

From the Latin *amatorculus* (a little, sorry lover).

"Colleagues of Dr. Schiff privately agreed that being dubbed 'the **amatorculist**' by the nursing staff was probably what had precipitated his unfortunate breakdown in the emergency room." *(compare **meupareunia**)*

ambeer /AM beer/ n • The spit-out juice from chewing tobacco.

"Being a bat boy was a dream come true for Jimmy, but he soon found that dodging the streams of **ambeer** in the dugout took a lot of practice." (*compare* *sputative*)

ambisinister /am bi SIN ist er/ adj • Lacking manual dexterity with both hands; having "two left hands."

[Latin *ambi* both + *sinister* left]

"Spencer, the airport baggage-handler, had the perfect job for someone as **ambisinister** as himself. He'd solved the problem of punching the time clock by holding his card in his teeth, but the mandatory coffee break still posed special hazards for him, and he kept a rubberized poncho in his locker for the occasion." (*compare* *looby*)

ambodexter /AM buh dex ter/ n • A corrupt juror; a juror who takes money from both sides.

"Carolyn pocketed the cash and shook her head in amazement: if she had known that being an **ambodexter** was so lucrative, she wouldn't have dodged jury duty all those years." (*compare* *boodler, ripesuck*)

amourette /am oor ET/ n • A petty or insignificant love affair.

"Edward Kleeger, titan of business and industry, was devastated when the dominatrix he wined and dined on weekends told him that she was moving on, saying: 'You were never more than an **amourette**, Ed, and not a very enjoyable one, at that.'" (*compare* *amatorculist*)

amplexus /am PLEX us/ n • The mating embrace of a toad or a frog.

From the endlessly descriptive world of biology comes this sparkler of a word. Since it is common enough to refer to a repulsive person as a toad, a figurative use for **amplexus** logically presents itself.

"The last thing I remembered from that evening was hiding in the men's room to escape the attentions of the vile Mrs. Flamm. Early the next morning I awoke in a strange bed with a terrible hangover, only to realize with horror that I was firmly caught in her **amplexus**."　　(*compare* **strene**)

amychesis /*am ik EE sis*/ n • Involuntary scratching of a partner's back during sex.

"As she daubed her wounds with peroxide in the motel bathroom, Charlotte cursed her luck for having taken a lover who suffered from **amychesis**, and began working on what she would tell her husband this time."

(*compare* **dyspareunia**)

anaclitic /*an uh KLIT ik*/ adj • 1) Overly dependent on others for emotional support. 2) Overly dependent on one's mother.

[Greek *ana* again, up, back + *klinein* to lean]

"Everyone warned Ellen that she was coddling her teenage son, but she just couldn't resist when he whined from bed for a sponge bath, and so his **anaclitic** dependency continued to deepen."

As she dries off her husband's tears,
Beth wrinkles her nose up and sneers,
"Not to be a critic,
*but you're still **anaclitic**,*
and your mother's been dead now for years."

(*compare* **rectopathic**)

anagapesis /*an uh gap EE sis*/ n • A loss of feelings for one formerly loved.

This is a terrible yet useful word. For all those who at one time or another have clumsily and ineffectually struggled to say, "I don't love you anymore," without having to actually *say* it, don't be fooled: "I *love* you, I'm just not *in* love with you" is a horrible thing to tell somebody. To avoid this and other clichés, it is better to tell one's ex-to-be that one has been stricken with **anagapesis**—then get the hell out of there before he or she reaches for the dictionary. (*compare **allorgasmia**, **anaxiphilia***)

anaphrodisiac /*an af ro DEE zhee ak*/ adj • Suppressing or eliminating sexual desire. n • Something that acts against sexual desire.

"The two women—both in their early thirties and utterly unattractive—scored a hit with their best-seller *The Drools*, which detailed everything women found **anaphrodisiac** about men." (*compare **ozoamblyrosis***)

anaxiphilia //*an AX if EEL ee uh*/ n • The act of falling in love with the wrong person.

Another in a long list of depressingly common human afflictions, **anaxiphilia** can befall anyone. While this word is not an insult *per se*, it can be used to gently rib—or brutally make fun of—someone who has recently had his or her heart crushed. (*compare **anagapesis***)

androgalactozemia /*AN dro gal AK toe ZEE mee uh*/ n • Secretion of milk from the male breast.

[Greek *andros* man + *gala* milk + *zemia* loss]
Could any creature be more deserving of ridicule than

the man with **androgalactozemia**? Probably not. The only consolation for the poor slob with this condition is that since most people don't believe such a thing can actually happen, when confronted with it they will probably be too perplexed to laugh, at least at first.

"A shortage of nondairy creamer threatened to disrupt the third annual **Androgalactozemia** Society luncheon, but the crisis was soon averted."

*(compare **gynecomastia, pogogniasis**)*

androphilic */an dro FIL ik/* adj • Preferring men over animals.

"Aunt Lucille was a gracious hostess, but she was getting on in years, so at tea everyone pretended not to notice the frenzied and insistent leg-humpings of Winston, her **androphilic** schnauzer."

*(compare **anthropozoophilic**)*

anhedonia */an hed O nee uh/* n • The inability to experience feelings of pleasure or happiness.

[*an* (neg.) + Greek *hedone* pleasure + *ia*]

As people with **anhedonia** are quite likely to make life miserable for everyone around them, this is a word worth knowing.

"Audrey surrendered to her **anhedonia** and married a shriveled and whining orthodontist. Why not? It was impossible for her to be happy anyway. At least this way she got full dental coverage." *(compare **antithalian**)*

anile */AN ile/* adj • Old-womanish.

"Montigew wanted very much to play with the other boys, but his attempts to throw a baseball were so **anile** that he wound up skipping rope with the girls again."

anililagnia /uh NIL ih LAG nee uh/ n • Sexual attraction to elderly women.

"Mortimer felt as though he was cursed by the gods: he had finally come to grips with his **anililagnia**, but now his lovers kept dying on him." (*compare **gerontophilia***)

anilingus /ay nil ING us/ n • Sexual contact between mouth and anus.

While this word may not be your cup of tea, **anilingus** is evidently enjoyed by enough people to warrant inclusion in a number of fine dictionaries.

"Melvin had always been the office brownnoser, but when the new management team arrived he stepped up his act to full-fledged **anilingus**." (*compare **lecheur***)

anility /uh NIL it ee/ n • Old-womanishness.

"After the candidate's disastrous performance on national television, it was Peterson's unenviable duty as campaign manager to remind him that **anility** was not what most people looked for in a leader."

animalist /AN im al ist/ n • A person who engages in bestiality.

"As a boxer, Hector 'The **Animalist**' Suarez was rather proud of his moniker, thinking that it doubtless made reference to some boundless crop of energy that he possessed. In reality, it stemmed more from his nightly habit of drinking himself insensate enough to couple with anything with a pulse." (*compare **anthropozoophilic, avisodomy***)

anisomastia /an iss o MAST ee uh/ n • The state of having breasts of unequal size.

animalist

"Hedda was sold on surgery for her **anisomastia**; the only question was whether to go for enlargement, reduction, or a little of both." (*compare* **macromastia, micromastia**)

ankyloproctia /an kil o PROK tee uh/ n • A severe constriction of the anus.

[Greek *ankylos* bent, crooked + *proktos* anus]

The perfect word to describe a tight-ass.

"Donald's **ankyloproctia** came as a terrible blow to the pudgy gourmand. His doctors had now restricted him to a diet consisting entirely of foods that could easily pass through his narrowed system, such as baby food and over-ripe bananas." (*compare* **sterky**)

anoia /uh NOY uh/ n • Idiocy.

Paradoxically, a condition most annoying to those who do not suffer from it.

anorchous /an OR kus/ adj • Having no testicles.

"'Had you not been such an **anorchous** jellyfish,' shrieked Sheila, Kevin's shrill and over-educated wife, '*you* would have gotten the promotion!'"

anorchus /an OR kus/ n • A man with no testicles.

"Only after the humiliating incident with the waiter did it finally dawn on Louisa that she had married a total **anorchus**." (*compare* **triorchid**)

anorgasmic /AN or GAZ mik/ adj • Failing to achieve orgasm during sex.

"While the **anorgasmic** relations he suffered with his fifth wife were not something Simon would have wished upon himself, they were certainly an improvement over the situation with his previous brides, all of whom had refused to sleep with him at all." (*compare* **dyspareunia**)

anteric //an TER ik/ adj • Seeking vengeance for slighted love.

"In an **anteric** rage, Sarah decided that slashing the tires of her ex-boyfriend's pickup truck just wasn't enough. So she set it ablaze and flung herself on top of it."

(*compare* **anaxiphilia**)

anthropozoophilic /AN thro PO zoo FILL ik/ adj • Attracted to both people and animals.

[Greek *anthropos* man + *zoon* animal + *philein* to love]

While this term is primarily employed to describe insects, we are confident that some of our more deviant readers will find another use for it.

"'Any port in a storm,' thought the **anthropozoophilic**

Edmund, after the third and last farmer's daughter rebuffed his licentious advances, and he was told in no uncertain terms to go and sleep in the barn."

(*compare **animalist, avisodomy, omnifutuant***)

antinomian /*an tee NOME ee an*/ n • A person who believes that faith in Christ frees him or her from moral and legal obligations.

"No one in his small Southern town objected to Lloyd not paying taxes, using a homemade license plate, or flying his own separatist flag proclaiming his trailer home/arsenal to be a 'principality of Jesus.' But there had to be a limit to religious expression, and when the zealous **antinomian** cut the ticket line at the high school football game, a lynching party quickly coalesced out of the throng."

(*compare **eisegetical, tartuffe***)

antithalian /*an tee THALE ee an*/ adj • Disapproving of laughter or festivity.

"Many citizens were distressed by the law-and-order mayor's **antithalian** crusade of ticketing anyone who laughed in public ('It's a quality-of-life issue,' he insisted). But no one could deny that the policy, when enforced, lent the city something of a genteel and cultivated air."

(*compare **anhedonia, cachinnator***)

antivitruvian /*an ti vit ROO vee an*/ adj • Taking pleasure in destroying architectural monuments.

This wonderfully specific word comes to us from the name of a famed Roman architect, Vitruvius. While it is unlikely that the reader will ever have an opportunity to rise at a town meeting and, raising his or her voice in a stentorian fashion, cry: "You, sir, are nothing more than a base and vile **antivitruvianist!**," it is still a word that every lover of fine buildings should know. Certainly there seem to be an inordinate number of these despicable creatures in circulation today.

"Once he promised them a fifty-dollar tax credit, most of the townsfolk came around to supporting the councilman's **antivitruvian** plan to rip down the seventeenth-century town hall and replace it with a new cinderblock courthouse."

(*compare* **grimthorpe**)

apistia /*uh PISS tee uh*/ n • Marital infidelity.

"Johann was a sly and crafty fellow: having inserted a clause in his prenuptial agreement asserting that **apistia** could not be considered grounds for alimony, he now was free to whore his way about town with complete abandon."

(*compare* **bedswerver**)

apodyopsis /*ap o die OP sis*/ n • The act of imagining someone naked.

"There were times, such as the summer he worked at the nursing home, when Wendell found his compulsive **apody-opsis** more of a curse than a blessing."

apoglutic /*ap o GLOO tik*/ adj • Having a tiny rump.

For those readers who prefer rear ends that are built for comfort and not for speed, the authors offer **apoglutic** for use as an insult.

"As a personal trainer to the stars, Rolanda was renowned for her ability to render anyone **apoglutic**. Indeed, she refused to consider a client a success until her posterior was skinny enough to make sitting on it decidedly uncomfortable."

(*compare* **kakopygian, unipygic**)

apophallation /ap o fal AY shun/ n • Among slugs, the practice of chewing off a partner's penis following sex.

Slugs are endowed with what is proportionately one of the largest penises in the animal kingdom; an eight-inch slug can have a member that is just as long as he is. There is a terrible downside to such phallic magnificence, however. Every so often a slug will get stuck. Imagine: you're hot and sweaty, the deed has been done, and you really want nothing so much as a cigarette and a shower, but your partner just can't withdraw. Can you really blame the slug for chewing it off?

"Mr. Duval was a dedicated, if slightly unstable, health teacher. Nevertheless, there was some degree of controversy among the local parents when he began showing nature films of animals engaging in **apophallation** to his sophomore class as a deterrent to sexual activity."

(*compare **dyspareunia***)

arrhenopiper /uh REN o pipe er/ n • "One that looks lewdly at men," as defined by Joseph T. Shipley in his *Dictionary of Early English*.

A word that well deserves resurrection.

"Cadwaller's buttocks clenched tightly, as they always did whenever he had to pass through the gaggle of boisterous **arrhenopipers** blocking the door to the men's room."

(*compare **gynopiper***)

artamesia /art uh MEE zhee uh/ n • Sexual dissatisfaction in a woman due to the premature climax of her partner.

It is a beautiful thing that a word exists for this all-too-common occurrence. There is a difference of opinion, however, as to where the word **artamesia** comes from. According to J.E. Schmidt, author of *The Lecher's Lexicon,* the roots are the Greek *artao* (to hang) and *mesos* (in the middle). While this explanation is both plausible and amusing, one cannot ignore the case to be made for Artimesia, the ancient Greek queen of Helicarnassus, as the eponymous root of the word.

According to the history books, Artimesia was exceedingly fond of a youth named Darnadus, and when he rebuffed her licentious advances she tore his eyes from his head as he slept (you go, girlfriend!!!). Yet a third possibility is that the word originates with Artemesia Gentileschi (1593–1653), a renowned Italian painter. Her most famous painting, *Judith and Maidservant with the Head of Holofernes,* happens to depict two women who have decapitated a man who has slept with one of them.

So there are three viable explanations—which hardly matters, really, for if you're experiencing **artamesia** you need more than a good etymology.

(*compare **acokoinonia, meupareunia***)

aspermia /*ay SPERM ee uh*/ n • Inability to ejaculate semen.

"Ironically, the very same **aspermia** that rendered Hedley's sexual efforts futile for him also led to his gaining a reputation as a tireless love machine."

(*compare **spermatoschesis***)

asshead /*ASS hed*/ n • A blockhead; a stupid person.

While **asshead** has the ring of a modern-day schoolyard taunt, it actually has a long and noble history as a legitimate insult. As such, it has a certain blunt and potent charm.

(*compare **lobcock***)

assot /*ASS ot*/ v • To make a fool of.

"Her first day at her first job out of college, and Kirsten

had thoroughly **assotted** herself. They'd told her to 'dress her best' for work, and so she had donned the only finery she had: her bright green prom dress from five years ago. Oh, the humiliation when they sent her home in tears!"

atolmia /ay TOLE mee uh/ n • Impotence in a man due to lack of confidence.

"Operating according to the credo 'You've got to break a man all the way down before you can build him up again,' the Longwell Institute for Male Pleasure (L.I.M.P.) racked up several successes—as well as a large number of spectacular failures—with its 'tough love' approach to curing **atolmia**." (*compare* **anorgasmic, peniculas**)

autosmia /aw TOZ mee uh/ n • The smelling of one's own bodily odors.

[Greek *auto* self + *osme* smell]

"Jared was an outcast his whole life, somehow never grasping that his erotic obsession with **autosmia** was part of the reason why." (*compare* **odorivector**)

autotheist /aw toe THEE ist/ n • One who believes that he or she is God.

"Fisk's many minions were accustomed to the billionaire **autotheist's** monstrous egotism. It was his complete neglect of even the most basic personal hygiene that took a bit more getting used to." (*compare* **pleionosis**)

avisodomy /uh VIZ o dome ee/ n • The act of having sex with a bird.

Live long enough and there will come a time when you desperately wish that you knew a word that means to have sex with a bird. Bereft of such knowledge, most people will sputter and cast about in vain before coming up with a colorful but crude expression, such as 'duck-fucker.'

Avisodomy covers sexual congress with any type of bird, but it is most commonly applied to fowl.

"Although they were the only house on campus that insisted their pledges be videotaped engaging in **avisodomy,** Sigma Tau Delta had such a degree of social cachet, and threw such splendid mixers, that they had more pledges clamoring to join than any other three fraternities combined." *(compare **animalist, anthropozoophilic**)*

axunge /AX *unj*/ n • Medicinal lard prepared from geese or pigs.

Good for what ails ye!

"Sales of the new minestrone soup did not benefit from the consumer group's announcement that 'natural flavorings' was really just a fancy name for **axunge.**"

*(compare **bezoar**)*

· B ·

baculum /*BAK yoo lum*/ n • The penis bone; present in many mammals, absent in humans.

Thank God.

"Although he traveled in the highest social circles, Tully was regarded as something of an eccentric, perhaps because of his extensive **baculum** collection."

badling /*BAD ling*/ n • A man who is effeminate or worthless.

[Old English *baedling* a womanish man]

"After the storm, all the women and children bailed desperately to keep the lifeboat from sinking. Not Lucas the **badling,** though. He just hopped up and down in the stern, flapping his arms in the air and exclaiming, 'Oh my, oh, my!'" (*compare* **subvirate**)

balanic /*buh LAN ik*/ adj • Having to do with the penis or clitoris.

"Sigmund E. Hopfeizer, M.D., was irked: didn't his generous donation to his alma mater warrant a slightly more prominent acknowledgment than a plaque in the Hall of **Balanic** Studies?"

balanoplasty /*buh LAN o plass tee*/ n • Plastic surgery of the penis.

"When his doctor enthusiastically recommended drastic **balanoplasty** to cure his slight incontinence, Arthur knew it was time to get a second opinion."

(compare **phalloplasty**)

barathrum /*BA rath rum*/ n • 1. An insatiable glutton. 2. An extortionist who will not be satisfied.

So called after the **Barathrum,** a pit outside the city of Athens into which criminals, alive and dead, were thrown.

(compare **gulchin, rabiator**)

baratress /*BA ruh tress*/ n • A female quarreler.

She may just as easily pick on a woman, but like her cousin the **agitatrix,** the **baratress** strikes a special fear into the heart of many a man. For who knows what comment, innocuous though it might seem, will raise the hackles and invoke the ire of a **baratress**? It could be something innocent, such as "That dress looks good on you," or it could

barathrum

be an incredibly stupid statement, like "I had lunch with my ex-girlfriend today."

(*compare* **agitatrix, breedbate, quibberdick**)

bariatrics /*barry AT rix*/ n, pl • The field of medicine concerned with obesity.

"As he lay on the floor of the sauna in his rubber suit, moments before lapsing into unconsciousness, Milton reflected that the science of **bariatrics** still had a long way to go." (*compare* **impinguinate**)

barkled /*BARK ld*/ adj • Encrusted with dirt; used especially to describe a person's skin.

"Rich though she was, Hetty still fancied that society owed her something, and she tried to bilk the state out of as much welfare as she could. There was always a mad rush to get her children looking as **barkled** and ill clad as possible each time the caseworker came to her door."

(*compare* **trugabelly**)

barlichood /*BAR lich ood*/ adj • Drunk and mean.

"All the regulars at McKenna's looked forward to seven o'clock with keen anticipation. For that was when old Mr. Gleason, thoroughly **barlichood** with cheap gin, would begin hollering with rage at the nightly news on the TV over the bar." (*compare* **debacchate, zowerswopped**)

barrator /*BA ruh tor*/ n • An ambulance-chasing lawyer.

Yes, there exists a time-honored term for this bottom-feeder.

There is nothing so nice
as a slick patch of ice
on the sidewalk

*to the **barrator.***
For ultimately, all misery
is useful for lining his pockets more.

With great indignation, and fury unbridled,
he gets you the monies to which you're entitled.
                    (*compare **bdelloid, leguleian, rabulistic***)

bastinado /*bass tin AY do*/ v • To beat the soles of someone's feet with a stick or club. n • The practice of beating the soles of the feet with a stick or club.

"Talk about dedication: Luigi worked full time during the week as flogger and executioner, but somehow still found time enough to take bastinado classes on the weekends." (*compare **ferule, pandy***)

bathetic /*buh THET ik*/ adj • Falsely sentimental.

"Samantha was truly sickened by the way her weasel-like boyfriend went to such great lengths to avoid taking the blame for anything, frequently waxing **bathetic** and crying crocodile tears. After one such episode too many, she dumped a pot of boiling spaghetti water on his foot and announced that she was leaving."

(*compare **rectopathic***)

bathycolpian /*bath ik ALL pee an*/ adj • Having deep cleavage.

There are so many banal expressions for this particular concept that our language is crying out for a resurrection of the proper terminology. Very few women out there enjoy the salutation "nice rack!" or relish compliments on their "bazookas." And while a statement like "Your **bathycolpian** state overwhelms and delights me" may not pave

bathycolpian

the way to romance on its own, at least it's less likely to get you slapped.

"There was a moment of confusion during the interview on the Capitol steps, when the senator's hearing aid fell down the front of the **bathycolpian** reporter's blouse."

*(compare **mammose**)*

bdellatomy /del AT o mee/ n • The cutting of a leech while it is sucking, in order to increase the flow of blood from the patient.

Apparently plain old leeching just wasn't disgusting enough to cure everybody.

"As a young surgeon, Clarence soon learned not to assign names to his leeches; it only made it harder for him when the time came for a **bdellatomy**."

bdelloid /DELL oid/ adj • Resembling a leech.

[Greek *bdella* leech + *oid*]

"Paige's **bdelloid** younger brother refused to get a job, arguing that he hadn't 'found the right thing yet.' Instead, he continued to siphon bed and board off of his friends and a roster of fleeting lovers." *(compare **barrator**)*

bdolotic /DOLL uh tik/ adj • Prone to farting.

What can we say about **bdolotic**, except that its usefulness as a word is obvious.

"To the horror of her hapless niece, old Mrs. Grubowski not only grew more and more violently drunk as the evening progressed, but increasingly **bdolotic**, as well."

*(compare **carminative**, **flatus**, **meteorism**)*

beadledom /BEE dul dum/ n • Petty and stupid officialdom.

Nonsensical rules stubbornly adhered to are one hallmark

of **beadledom,** the culture of which is seemingly always expanding. But **beadledom** is not just about red tape. It is a state of mind: the standard mode of thinking for most of the lazy, stupid, mean, and self-important people who staff our bureaucracies.

"The insufferable **beadledom** of the snotty teenage parking-lot attendant made Joyce see red. After reparking her pickup truck five times within the white lines—each time somehow unsatisfactorily—she grimly backed up over his little hut in revenge." (*compare* **spuddle**)

beau-nasty /*bow NASS tee*/ n • A slovenly fop.

The correlation between vanity and personal hygiene is sometimes a tenuous one.

"Armand the **beau-nasty** was almost ready for his blind date. He donned his wrinkled but expensive shirt, slipped on his malodorous Italian shoes, and admired his reflection in the mirror. Noticing a clot of spackling compound in his hair, he donned a fedora at a rakish angle and strutted out the door." (*compare* **muscod**)

bedizen /*bee DIZ en*/ v • To dress in a flashy or vulgar manner.

[*be-+ dizen* to dress gaudily]

"Most of the time, our aunt Martha was a quietly unattractive person. When fully **bedizened** for a special occasion, however, such as one of her semiannual dates with the local knacker, she transformed into a scarecrowlike monstrosity." (*compare* **callomaniac, mab**)

bedswerver / *BED swerv er*/ n • An unfaithful spouse.

A more visually expressive term for a cheating mate is hard to find. **Bedswerver** conjures up the image of a husband or wife walking toward the conjugal bed, then at the last possible moment thinking "Naaah," and changing direction midstride. (*compare* **apistia**)

bedung /*bee DUNG*/ v • 1) To cover with shit. 2) To daub with shit.

There are many words in English having to do with excremental matter, but it is rare to come across one with such delicate shadings of meaning. Useful for describing everything from the object that has been daubed with the lightest and most gauzy shadings of ordure to the farmer who has had his fertilizer tractor overturn on him, **bedung** is special. (*compare* **bemute, bepiss, bespawled, bevomit**)

begrutten /*bee GROO ten*/ adj • Having one's face swollen or disfigured from weeping.

[*be-+ grutten* (past participle of *greet,* meaning to weep)]

"Shortly after the evangelist was indicted for fraud, his fleshy and perpetually **begrutten** wife began appearing regularly on television, exhorting the faithful to pray for a mistrial." (*compare* **plorabunde, rectopathic**)

beldam /*BELL dam*/ n • A mean and ugly old woman.

"Bartholemew was blessed with scant physical courage: in fact, he lived in constant fear of the **beldam** across the hall with the yippy poodle." (*compare* **grimalkin**)

bemute /*bee MUTE*/ v • To drop dung on from above, as does a bird.

When compiling a book of odd English words, it never hurts to throw in one or two denoting the act of dropping shit on someone from a considerable height.

"In a move that was arguably more mentally unbalanced

than it was cunning, Gallhager had finally found the perfect way to avoid traffic tickets when he ventured into the city. Each night he would park his car directly under the lamppost where all the pigeons sat; after several weeks, no traffic agent in the world would go near his **bemuted** vehicle." (*compare **feculent***)

bepiss /*bee PISS*/ v • To urinate upon; to wet with urine.

No surprises as far as the definition of this word is concerned.

"As headmaster of the boarding academy for troublesome children with parents of means, Quimby didn't fall for any of that namby-pamby, New Age, spare-the-rod business. When little Richie Snead **bepissed** his bed, he stripped the lad down to his undies, painted his face black, and forced him to parade in front of the student body carrying a sign reading, 'I Am a Filthy Little Bastard.'" (*compare **pissburnt***)

beray /*bee RAY*/ v • To splatter with feces.

"After getting **berayed** yet again, Ted the zookeeper made a grim vow: one day he would get even with those damn monkeys." (*compare **bescumber, conskite,***
*(**immerd, ordurous, sharny, shitten***)

bescumber /*bee SCUM ber*/ v • To splatter with feces; to spray with ordure.

This graphic, horrible-sounding verb is often applicable in life. Remember the bathroom stall in Grand Central Station that time you absolutely *couldn't* wait? Was it not **bescumbered** from floor to eye level, challenging your knowledge of human anatomy and/or the laws of physics?
(*compare **beray, conskite,***
*immerd, ordured, sharny, shitten***)

beslobber /*bee SLOB er*/ v • To cover with sloppy kisses. Also, to befoul with spittle or anything else running from the mouth.

That covers everything from orange juice to—well, more exotic liquids.

"Balthazar reached to his pocket, then groaned inwardly: why was it that he could never remember to bring a spare handkerchief on these dates with his **beslobbering** new girlfriend Estelle?" (*compare* **conspue**)

bespawled /*bee SPALD*/ adj • Spattered with saliva.

This is another of the infamous *be*-words (**bevomit, bepiss**, etc.) that add so much color to our language.

"As part of the republic's new 'war on corruption,' public officials convicted of accepting bribes were forced to run a gauntlet of angry citizens while naked. While running, they were exposed to the most hideous **bespawling** imaginable." (*compare* **screable, sialismus**)

bespew /*bee SPEW*/ v • To eject vomit upon.

"It was another one of those nights for the Jenkinses: getting drunk, fighting viciously, making up, making love, and, inevitably, **bespewing** each other before it was all over."

(*compare* **tumbrel**)

bevomit /*bee VOM it*/ v • To vomit upon.

There are two cardinal rules where **bevomiting** is concerned. 1) It is better to **bevomit** someone other than yourself. 2) Never **bevomit** someone larger than you.

In his *Dictionary of the Vulgar Tongue*, Sir Francis Grose lists a wonderful phrase for the **bevomiter**: Admiral of the Narrow Seas ("one who from drunkenness vomits into the lap of the person sitting opposite to him").

(*compare* **emetomaniac, hyperemian**)

bespew

bezoar /*BEE zore*/ n • A hardened hair ball found in the digestive tracts of grazing animals, sometimes rumored to have medicinal use.

Every man of the world should have a few of these lying around—perhaps for use as paperweights.

"On the steppes of Old Mother Russia we had no baseballs, but more than once of an afternoon we would go out and toss the old **bezoar** around."   (*compare* ***coproma***)

bilious /*BILL ee us*/ adj • Suffering from an overflow of bile from the liver, with symptoms including headache, indigestion, furry tongue, and lethargy.

"Fifteen straight nights of drinking had resulted in the superintendent's present **bilious** condition—he was definitely in no shape to clean the sewer drain."

(*compare **crapulent***)

bivirist /*BIH vir ist*/ n • A woman who enjoys sex with two men at the same time.

"Was the electorate more concerned with her stand on the issues, or were such revelations simply less damaging to a politician with a *conservative* record? Whatever the reason, the candidate's salad days as a confirmed **bivirist** never became a major issue in her campaign." (*compare **trollism***)

blatherskite /*BLATH er skite*/ n • A boaster; a loudmouth. A blathering fellow.

"'Simmer down, you **blatherskites**!' yelled the cathouse madam at the posse of rowdy, whiskey-soaked cowboys in her waiting room. 'The next one of y'all starts trouble I swear won't be able to piss for a week without hollerin'!'"

(*compare **cacafuego, ventose***)

blattoid /*BLAT oid*/ adj • Resembling a cockroach.

"Duane was a legend as an exterminator, in part because he could really think like those he was hired to kill, and as the years rolled on he became more and more **blattoid** himself." (*compare **suoid***)

blennorrhea /*blen uh REE uh*/ n • The morbid and excessive secretion of mucus.

When every corner of every tissue in the house has been

used twice, the toilet paper is ancient history, the sore area under your nose resembles a pink toothbrush moustache, and your nostrils are plugged with wads of shredded dinner napkin, then you know that **blennorrhea** is upon you.

(*compare **snurt***)

blissom /*BLISS um*/ v • To copulate with a ewe; said of rams (and, less frequently, shepherds). adj • In heat; ready to be **blissomed.**

blissom

This little charmer sounds like it should mean something sweet and ethereal, like "blossom" or "blessing," and perhaps it does, in its own way. However, if one reads in the culture section of the paper about a "**blissoming** young talent on the downtown arts scene," one may be reasonably if not entirely sure that a printing error is to blame.

"Having **blissomed** the ewe, Calvert found himself strangely devoid of any hint of remorse." (*compare* **brim**)

blowmaunger /BLOW *mong er*/ n • A person who is fat to the point that his or her cheeks are puffed out.

"Climbing up the long flight of stairs leading to his podiatrist's office was always a strenuous chore for Chester the **blowmaunger**. Today it was harder than ever for him to catch his breath, what with his cheeks being full of chunks of chocolate éclair. Only the prospect of those root-beer-flavored lollipops at the top gave him the determination to press on." (*compare* **brephopolysarcia, porknell, pursy**)

blowze /BLOUZE/ n • "A fat, red flaccid bloted [sic] wench, or one whose whole head is dressed like a slattern." (Nathaniel Bailey's *Dictionary of the English Tongue*, 1761.)

"For those magical ten minutes, the inexorable march of time rolled back for the boozy old **blowze** in the hotel piano bar, as she warbled along mistily to the strains of her sentimental favorite, 'Send in the Clowns.'"

bolus /BO *lus*/ n • A ball of chewed food, ready to be swallowed. Also, something hard to swallow, such as a big pill.

"The enormous **bolus** in his cheek oscillated slightly as he spoke, but Cleon showed no sign of getting ready to swallow it and continued his lengthy monologue."

bonnyclabber /*BON ee klab er*/ n • Milk gone sour; thickened, curdled milk. Also, beer mixed with buttermilk or sour cream.

Bonnyclabber comes from the Irish *bainne* (milk) + *claba* (thick mud). One sees the word shortened to *clabber,* with no change in meaning. Milk that has turned is said to be *clabrous.*

"Experimentation proved beyond a doubt what Winston had suspected all along: pounding down mugfuls of **bonnyclabber** was not an effective hangover remedy."

(*compare* **caseation**)

boodler /*BOOD ler*/ n • One who happily accepts or offers bribes.

"Busted while trying to purchase an illegal substance in Mexico City, Maurice was sure that his political career had come to an end. But in a happy twist of fate, the judge turned out to be an agreeable old **boodler** who was willing to forget about the whole episode in exchange for a small honorarium." (*compare* **cacique, ripesuck**)

borborygmus /*bor bor IG muss*/ n • A rumbling in the intestines caused by gas.

"Andy, the chaplain, was a true professional, and when the sacred silence of the prayer circle was shattered by the severe **borborygmus** of one of his flock, he continued with his benediction without missing a beat."

(*compare* **flatus**)

brachyphallic /*BRAK ee FAL ik*/ adj • Having a penis that is very short.

"Swineburne, the **brachyphallic** customs agent, closed his eyes and began to inwardly chant his personal mantra,

'It ain't the size of the boat, it's the motion of the ocean,' as he removed his boxer shorts and entered into his newly-wed's embraces for the first time."

(compare **macromaniac, micropenis, peniculas, subvirate**)

breedbate /BREED bate/ n • One looking for a fight or argument; a troublemaker.

All families have at least one **breedbate**—he or she who insists on talking politics over Thanksgiving dinner, or who gives unwanted advice on whether to circumcise a newborn. What is one to do? For starters, it might pay to become familiar with some of the words in this book. Because if an argument is unavoidable, one might as well get some good digs in. (compare **baratress, quibberdick**)

brephopolysarcia /BREPH o pol ee SAR shuh/ n • Excessive fleshiness in an infant.

[Greek *brephos* newborn infant + *poly* many + *sarx* flesh]

All babies are fat. Fat little cheeks, fat little fingers, fat little toes. It helps make them cute, which is the only reason their parents put up with them. (After all, they just cry most of the time, and realistically speaking they won't be good for any kind of heavy labor for at least several years.) For the most part, people seem to love these fat little people, but every once in a while one comes across babies with **brephopolysarcia** that is so striking one has to recoil in horror and wonder: Do even their *parents* think they're cute?

(compare **bulchin**)

brim /BRIM/ v • To be in heat. Also, to copulate (said of swine).

"With a deep feeling of pride and satisfaction, Larsen inhaled the fresh morning air and surveyed his little farm:

the cows lowing in the fields, the sheep grazing on the hill, the swine **brimming** furiously in their pens."

*(compare **blissom**)*

brochity /*BROCH it ee*/ n • Crookedness of the teeth.

[Latin *brocchitas* a projection of the teeth in animals]

"As the headmistress of the Sterling Thrush Academy for Young Ladies, Wilma Thackleberry prided herself on her ability to transform even the least refined young woman into a paragon of charm. But when she was confronted with Edna, she of the **brochity** grimace (and fat ankles to boot), she simply told the girl to keep her mouth closed at all times and always wear long pants."

*(compare **gubbertush**)*

bromidrosiphobia /*bro mih dro sif O bee uh*/ n • A hallucinatory fear of body odor.

One of only four phobias included in this book (out of a possible five hundred or more). **Bromidrosiphobia** is interesting because it carries with it the odd notion of olfactory hallucinations. Just what does one do with a **bromidrosiphobe**—shake him by the shoulders and tell him he's smelling things again? *(compare **muscod, stinkard**)*

bromidrosis /*bro mid RO sis*/ n • Ill-smelling sweat.

"Russell never quite made the big time as a professional wrestler, his trick of overcoming opponents with his **bromidrosis** apparently failing to captivate audiences."

*(compare **kakidrosis, maschalephidrosis, podobromhidrosis**)*

bromomenorrhea /*BRO mo men o REE uh*/ n • Foulsmelling menstrual discharge.

Vile, loathsome, and until now, unmentionable.

"The day they started advertising **bromomenorrhea** remedies during the evening news, Mr. Pendleton finally threw his television away."   (*compare **stomatomenia***)

bromopnea /*bro MOP nee uh*/ n • Foul-smelling breath.

"Dr. Hubbard was a bit of a mystery to us at the clinic: as a dentist he was a genius with a drill, yet he couldn't seem to cure his own horrid **bromopnea**."

(*compare **saprostomus***)

buccula /*BUK yoo luh*/ n • A loose, saggy mass of flesh underneath the chin; a double chin.

"Many were the tossings and turnings that night in the Carpathian village, as the sleepless peasants cowered in their beds from fear of becoming the next victim of the evil Count **Buccula**, world's portliest vampire."

(*compare **choller***)

bulchin /*BULCH in*/ n • A chubby or broad-faced boy.

"Everyone loved Jimmie, the class **bulchin** with a limp. Most of the boys expressed their affection by throwing mud at him, or by taking turns kicking him in the rear end."   (*compare **brephopolysarcia***)

burke /*BURK*/ v • To murder by smothering; originally, in order to sell the corpse to a medical school.

So called after William Burke, the diabolical nineteenth-century Edinburgh killer who suffocated his victims and sold their unblemished corpses to medical schools for dissection.

Also, figuratively, to "kill" something quietly or furtively behind the scenes: to **burke** an investigation, for example.

burke

byental /*by ENT ull*/ n • A horse's penis.

Or, as the *Oxford English Dictionary* puts it: "The yard of a horse."

This word is hereby brought to your attention so you don't end up ordering the fricasseed **byental** while on your eating tour of provincial England (at least not without being fully informed). (*compare pizzle*)

byspel /*BY spel*/ n • The outcast of a family.

"The **byspel** of his rich and landed clan, young Norton lived alone in a shed, by the woods on the edge of the estate. He was not invited to meals, and never spoken to. He did not receive an allowance, an education, or familial love of any kind. He prowled about mostly at night, subsisting on roots and the thin gruel put out for the hogs. He wore homespun clothing. And after the big house burned to the ground, taking everyone with it, he inherited every penny of the family fortune." (*compare uzzard*)

byental

· C ·

cacafuego /*kak uh FWAY go*/ n • A braggart; literally, a "shit-fire."

[Spanish *caca* shit + *fuego* fire]

"The drinks kept on coming, and Boris the **cacafuego** continued with his loud, boastful tirades and vulgar gesticulations. No matter; he was about to get his comeuppance—in the form of the beating of his life—from the little old lady quietly sipping her sherry at the end of the bar: the one with the brick in her purse."

*(compare **blatherskite, ventose**)*

cachinnator /*KAK in ate or*/ n • One who laughs loudly, excessively, or for no reason.

[Latin *cachinnare* to laugh aloud]

Unfortunately, one of the more necessary words in this lexicon. **Cachinnation** can arise anywhere, at any time, and it is always extremely irritating. Of all the everyday sensory assaults whose source is one's fellow human being, perhaps only a powerful bodily odor is less agreeable than the noise made by the **cachinnator**.

This infernal pest, along with his latest unholy mutation, the **cachinnator** on the cell phone, typically favors enclosed public spaces where many people are gathered together and from which escape is not possible. Who among us has been so lucky as to have not—and recently—cast baleful glances in the vicinity of some shrill and persistent **cachinnator** in our restaurant, theater, bus, or plane?

"Six hours trapped in a car with his **cachinnating,** slightly senile mother-in-law were enough to completely unhinge poor Morton, and he began to tear out his hair in great clumps."   (*compare **klazomaniac***)

cacique /*kuh SEEK*/ n • A corrupt and small-time Latin American political boss.

"United Banana's business motto, 'Find a good **cacique** and stick with him,' was hugely successful and widely imitated in its time."   (*compare **boodler, ripesuck***)

cacocallia /*kak o KAL ee uh*/ n • The state of being ugly but sexy.

Warning: The authors strongly advise against using this word as a compliment.   (*compare **gaucy***)

cacozelot /*kak o ZEL ut*/ n • An evil zealot.

"'One needs to be a bit of a **cacozelot** to succeed in this line of business,' explained Eric's seedy but avuncular supervisor at the fly-by-night investment firm, showing him to his very own cubicle. The young hiree began to feel that he had finally found a home."

cadator /*CAD uh tor*/ n • A beggar who poses as a decayed gentleman.

"Perhaps it was the shambling old beggar's graying temples, which lent him an air of faded dignity, or the tattered suit that had seen better days. Whatever the reason, Angie's heart was touched to the tune of a twenty-dollar bill. Unbeknownst to her, this **cadator's** carefully cultivated aura not only paid for a condo in Miami, but for a grow-ing collection of rare cartoon art as well."

(compare **mumblecrust, screeve**)

cagamosis /*kag uh* MO *sis*/ n • An unhappy or unpleasant marriage.

Considering how common the thing is which it describes, it is surprising that the word **cagamosis** is not more widely known. Alas, even divorce lawyers, the particular group that

cagamosis

transforms the misfortunes of unhappy marriages into fortunes for themselves, are probably overwhelmingly ignorant of the very word that lines their larders.

(compare synechthry)

callipygian /*kal ip EYE gee an*/ adj • Having nicely shaped buttocks.

From the Greek *kallos* (beautiful) + *pyge* (buttocks).

The noun form of this word is **callipyge** (a person with nicely shaped buttocks).

(compare dasypygal, pygobombe, steatopygous)

callomaniac /*kal o MAY nee ak*/ n • A person under the delusion that he or she is beautiful.

A true sparkler of a word. **Callomaniacs** are common enough, and often painfully easy to spot. They also belong to that peculiar group of people who one doesn't know whether to pity or to despise.

Excepting those few **callomaniacs** with hearts of gold (in whom, beauty being subjective, such self-deception is almost excusable), everyone with this condition should be ridiculed without mercy until cured.

"Ever the **callomaniac**, Gretchen insisted on squeezing her figure, with its grotesque marshmallow-like consistency, into a variety of overly tight pieces of spandex clothing, with the unfortunate result that large pockets of flesh would invariably spill out in bits and pieces."

(compare plutomaniac, sophomaniac)

cantabank /*KANT uh bank*/ n • A second-rate singer of ballads.

As everyone who has listened to top-40 radio understands, **cantabank** is still a useful word today.

callomaniac

cantabank

"As a manager of **cantabanks,** Murray felt a wave of validation as his latest protégé rose steadily up through the pop charts. All those months scouring mini-mall parking lots for 'that' kid, the one with the piercings and natural sneer that cried out 'Star,' had all been worth it."

*(compare **windbroach**)*

caprylic */kuh PRILL ik/* adj • Evocative of a rank and fetid goat (said of smells).

"Brush in hand and tears in his eyes, Horatio made a mental note not to let the hardware store man talk him into buying **caprylic** paint ever again." *(compare **hircine, rammish**)*

carminative */kar MIN uh tiv/* adj • Relieving flatulence; acting to expel wind from the body. n • An agent that relieves flatulence by helping to expel wind from the body.

caprylic

"Doug was talking to his pretty young boss when two things happened: the **carminative** prescribed for his indigestion took hold, and the elevator broke down."

(*compare* **bdolotic, flatus, meteorism**)

caseate /KAY *see ate*/ v • To become cheesy; be subject to **caseation**.

When someone asks you what you think of the new best-seller you wasted good money buying, tell them the book **caseates** in the second half, and you might feel a bit better. (*compare **bonnyclabber***)

caseation /*kay see AY shun*/ n • Conversion into cheese. Also, a morbid condition whereby flesh develops a cheesy appearance and consistency.

As with **caseate,** the best way to employ this potentially useful word is to think of "cheesy" as meaning crummy, corny, and tacky. Then you can apply **caseation** not only to substances like curd and flesh (ugh), but to things that deeply offend all amateur culture critics, such as screenplays that undergo a rapid and thorough process of **caseation** after being purchased by major Hollywood studios.

catagelophobe /*cat uh GELL o fobe*/ n • One who is pathologically fearful of being teased.

If you can't make fun of someone with a devastating social illness, who *can* you make fun of?

"Max, the stuttering **catagelophobe,** was hiding in the back of the bus as usual when on board came his worst nightmare: a troop of smart-alecky fourth-graders. Lunging for the emergency brake, he fled the conveyance in a state of high anxiety." (*compare **rectopathic***)

catarolysis /*kat uh RALL ih sis*/ n • The practice of cursing to let off steam.

"Denied the outlet of a prolonged **catarolysis** when things went wrong, Blake had a massive stroke and died shortly after making the amazing career switch from truck driver to beloved host of a live children's television show." (*compare **coprolalia***)

cepivorous /*sep IV or us*/ adj • Feeding on onions.

"Jeanie couldn't stop crying at the funeral, not so much out of grief for the deceased—indeed, she had hardly known him—as because she was seated next to her **cepivorous** uncle Bela." (*compare **ranivorous***)

ceruminosis /*SEH roo min O sis*/ n • The excessive secretion of **cerumen** (ear wax).

"Davey's parents breathed a sigh of relief: the sullen behavior, the bad grades, the loud music—**ceruminosis,** not Satan worship, was to blame." (*compare **gound0***)

chankings /*CHAN kings*/ n, pl • Slightly masticated spat-out food, such as olive pits or gristle.

Chankings are a part of life, and it is high time they

were recognized as such. The stubborn refusal of hosts and hostesses to provide suitable receptacles for their guests' **chankings** is a mark of careless incivility, even boorishness. After all, who feels comfortable balling up napkin after napkin of herring bones and sunflower seed husks? At the next function you attend, request a bowl for **chankings** in a polite and debonair fashion, and when one is delivered you'll be able to dispose of your cherry pits with an air of impeccable cultivation.

chaterestre /CHAT er EST er/ n • A woman who talks too much; a female chatterer.

That rarest of birds, the woman who talks too much, is a creature shrouded in legend and rarely, if ever, seen. Dim reports from faraway lands will occasionally arise, much akin to those concerning the yeti or the giant killer sloth of South America. Almost inevitably these stories are proven false by even the most casual examination. However, in the extremely unlikely event that the reader should happen upon this chimera, it will perhaps prove useful to be familiar with the correct terminology with which to describe her.   (*compare* ***clatterfart***)

chichiface /CHI chi face/ n • A person with a pinched and bony face.

It is always good to have another word at your disposal with which to describe a pinched and bony face, but the history of this word is more interesting than its definition. It is derived from the French *chichefache* (ugly, thin face). In English literature of the 1300s and 1400s, the *Chichevache* was the name of a fabled monster, perpetually hungry and starved due to the fact that it lived entirely on a diet of patient wives. (Not to be confused with the Bicorne, another fabled monster, which grew fat due to its diet of patient husbands.) (*compare* **scrag**)

chiromaniac /*KAI ro MAY nee ak*/ n • A compulsive masturbator.

"The truth was that Jeb Purdy had been injured in a freak yachting accident over the summer holiday. But the vicious gossip at school held that he was a **chiromaniac** whose parents had wrapped his hands in bandages to prevent him from abusing himself in class."

(*compare* **peotillomania, sacofricosis**)

cholagogic /*kall uh GOG ik*/ adj • Producing a flow of bile.

With a little liberty of usage, this medical term can be applied to such diverse phenomena as newpaper editorials, traffic jams, and modern architecture. (*compare* **bilious**)

choller /*CHALL er*/ n • Fat, pendulous flesh hanging from the lower jaw; double chin.

"Every morning the same dilemma for Mr. Pinkerton, the overnourished banker: should he button his collar above or below his massive **choller**?" (*compare* **buccula**)

chordee /*kore DEE*/ n • Painful downward curving of the erect penis, happening especially at night; sometimes a side effect of gonorrhea.

Also known as *phallocamposis*.

"Jenkins, the portly exhibitionist, might never have been picked out of the police lineup had his severe **chordee** not given him away." (*compare* **priapism**)

chrematisophiliac /*KREM uh tiz o FEEL ee ak*/ n • One who gets aroused from being charged money for sex.

In the vast pantheon of bizarre human sexual predilections, there are more than a few that can be hazardous to one's health. None, however, are as potentially damaging to the *wallet* as **chrematisophilia.**

"How sad that the union of this perfect couple was doomed to fail. They had so much in common—perhaps *too* much, for they were both **chrematisophiliacs,** and trading money back and forth just didn't 'do it' for either of them." (*compare **proxenetism***)

chyme /KIME/ n • Partially digested liquid food.

"Rosemary's filthy-drunk roomate had ruined yet another dish with her careless vomitings: after all, the recipe called for parsley, sage, and *thyme,* not **chyme.**" (*compare **lientery***)

cicisbeo /sih SIZZ bee o/ n • The young male lover/escort/admirer of a married woman.

Basically, a **cicisbeo** is the paramour of a married lady, although the definition is imprecise. Italian in origin, the word covers the spectrum of male admirers, from occasional hangers-on to full-fledged lovers.

circumstantiality /SUR cum STANCH ee AL it ee/ n • The inability to separate important from unimportant details when telling a story.

This psychiatric condition is often associated with symptoms such as confusion, a glazed stare, drooling, and narcolepsy. Not among the sufferers themselves, mind you, but those forced to listen to them.

claqueur /klak IRRH/ n • A member of a **claque** (a mob of hired applauders). Also, figuratively, any sycophantic yesman.

Whether they get money or just free tickets, it doesn't matter—**claqueurs** are the mainstay of infomercials and insipid little talk shows. Do they have no shame?

(compare *saulie*)

clarty-paps /CLAR tee paps/ n • A dirty, slovenly wife.

"Being a door-to-door salesman was not as glamorous and carefree as Saunders had pictured it. There had to be something more to life than hawking roach traps to **clartypapses** with their hair in curlers."

clatterfart /KLAT er fart/ n • A chatterer.

Clatterfart is one of those words that sound a bit worse than they really are. Such words come in handy when one wants to make someone feel bad but can't find anything particularly distasteful about him or her. One should never let such trivial obstacles discourage one from being insulting.

(compare *chaterestre*)

clinomaniac /KLY no MANE ee ak/ n • One suffering from an excessive desire to stay in bed.

"When the duchess spent a week of her Mediterranean holiday locked up in her hotel room ordering room service, her retinue feared she had become a **clinomaniac**. Only when they caught a glimpse of her virile new paramour through the keyhole did they stop worrying."

(compare *dysania*)

clyster /KLY ster/ v • To administer an enema. n • An enema.

"Paul's penchant for administering irrigations on the flimsiest pretense led to his being dubbed 'the **clyster** meister' by his fellow nurses."

(compare *huskanoy*)

clyster

cockalorum /*kok uh LO rum*/ n • A self-important little man.

"Strutting to and fro in his starched, resplendent little uniform with the plumes on the cap, his pencil mustache quivering as he squeaked redundant orders in a voice even the lowliest private was trained to ignore, the general's **cockalorum** nephew really made quite a spectacle. Unfortunately, as he himself was beginning to realize, he was extremely unlikely to survive the next coup."

(*compare* **beadledom, spuddle**)

collywobbles /*KALL ee wob ulls*/ n, pl • Intestinal distress characterized by cramping and diarrhea.

cockalorum

"Not a working bathroom in the whole department store, and a severe case of the **collywobbles:** Parker had to get creative—fast!" (*compare **lask, wamble***)

colpoxerosis /kole po zeh RO sis/ n • extreme dryness of the vagina.

Another medical term with its uses in everyday life.

"Vivian was immediately removed as editor of the school newspaper when officials caught wind of her upcoming article: Overcoming **Colpoxerosis** on Prom Night—What Every Girl Needs to Know."

(*compare **vaginismus***)

comprachico /KOM *pruh* CHEEK *o*/ n • A villain who sells children after first deforming them.

Before casting judgment on the **comprachico**, let the reader look deep within his own soul. For is it not possible that this man is merely trying to make ends meet? Perhaps he wrestled long and hard with his conscience before gravely announcing to his harried wife and three hungry children one night over a nearly empty dinner table: "I've decided to take that **comprachico** job Jim offered me down in the village."

(*compare **dippoldism***)

conky /KONK *ee*/ n • A person with a big nose.

Some sources nominate **conky** as a possible root of the pejorative term *honky*, meaning a white person.

"Sir Grossbeak had always been extremely proud of his immense honker; he even had his portrait painted in profile to show it off. When a falconing mishap cost him his prized appendage, he commissioned a magnificent prosthesis to be carved from an elephant's tusk."

(*compare **rhinoplast***)

conskite /*kun* SKITE/ v • To besplatter with dung.

"Darius, creative director of the Circus Maximus, sighed dejectedly: all the mobs ever wanted was blood,

blood, and more blood. Why, even his attempt to inject comedy into the show by having the Christians **conskited** by wild animals had flopped miserably."

(*compare **beray, bescumber,**
immerd, ordured, sharny, shitten)*

conspue /*kun SPEW*/ v • To spit on with contempt.

"As he stood on line for yet another unemployment check, Pendleton sighed and once again reflected that **conspuing** his boss's wife had been something of a miscalculation."
(*compare **sputative**)*

contrectation /*kon trek TAY shun*/ n • Touching and fingering, as in the initial stages of lovemaking. Also, a pathological urge to fondle all members of the opposite sex.

Contrectation describes the same root action (touching) in two very different contexts: primarily associated with tender lovers, the word moonlights in conjunction with drooling sex maniacs.

"As if Julius's **contrectation** weren't frustrating enough to deal with on its own, after the skiing accident he was confined to a full body cast and attended to by a squadron of buxom young nurses." (*compare **suppalpation**)*

copracrasia /*KOPE ruh KRAY zhuh*/ n • Involuntary defecation.

"Like it or not, it was **copracrasia** that set Merdy, the famous baggy-pants comedian, on his road to fame and fortune." (*compare **encopresis**)*

copremesis /*kope rem EE sis*/ n • The condition of being so constipated that one vomits one's own feces.

Sorry, but **copremesis** is not a word for the weak of stomach. When confronted with this little sparkler, most people say something like "No! That can't happen!" Well, it can happen, and does. The mere thought is enough to make even the most hardened logophiles put down their forks. So when you go to bed tonight, give thanks to the god of your choice that it hasn't happened to you.

(compare **allochezia**)

coprolagnia /KOPE ro LAG nee uh/ n • Erotic gratification from handling or smelling feces.

"In her third year of medical school, Lisa finally yielded to her latent **coprolagnia** and signed up for several courses in proctology."

contrectation

coprolalia /*kope ruh LAY lee uh*/ n • Pathological indecency of language; also, sexual gratification from indecent language.

"Claiming that his **coprolalia** was an affliction, not merely a bad habit, Swanson sued and regained his post as headmaster of the boarding school."

(*compare* **catarolysis**)

coprolite /*KOP ro lite*/ n • Fossilized dung.

The next time you cross swords with an elderly paleontologist you'll be glad to have this word in your verbal quiver.

coprolith /*KOP ruh lith*/ n • A hardened ball of excrement.

"At majestic Stoolhenge, one can gasp in awe at the massive **coprolith** monuments of a lost civilization."

coproma /*cop RO muh*/ n • A large clump of compacted feces that can form in the rectum, resembling a tumor.

"Having attended several medical seminars some years in the past, Dorland thought himself up to the task of rectifying his own **coproma** and made an ill-advised attempt at home, with the help of a mirror, some olive oil, and a pair of pinking shears."

(*compare* **scybalous**)

coprophagous /*ko PROF uh gus*/ adj • Dung-eating.

A person who eats dung is a **coprophagist**.

"Billy, the **coprophagous** circus dwarf, was always a big hit with the crowds, gamely trotting along in the wake of the trained ponies and disposing of what they left behind in his own special way—and always with a smile and a flourish." (*compare* **merdivorous, rhypophagous, scatophagous, stercovorous**)

coprophiliac /ko pro FILL ee ak/ n • A sexual deviant with an abnormal interest in feces.

Another word that, while perfectly offensive and usable in its own right, can also easily be used in a figurative sense.

"The politician gave a speech that night which many insiders considered to be the best of his career, in which he derided the press as 'nothing more than a bunch of bloodsucking **coprophiliacs.**'"   (*compare* ***coprolagnia***)

cotquean /KOT kween/ n • A man who involves himself overmuch in women's affairs; used disparagingly.

Cotquean is Anglo-Saxon for "house woman": *cot* (small house) + *quean* (woman). It owes its sting as a term of derision to the entrenched belief that men and women have their proper respective roles; as this belief comes under attack, the word loses some bite. Even so, we shall probably never see the day when men assume the mantle of **cotquean** with pride.   (*compare* ***badling, dammarel***)

crackheaded /KRAK hed ed/ adj • Crazy.

Although it certainly looks to be of contemporary coinage, **crackheaded** actually has a pedigree that far precedes the 1980s. There does not seem to be any direct relationship between the terms of then and now. Rather, *crackhead* appears to be a case of a new word arising in the form of an old and venerable one.

(*compare* ***mattoid***)

crapulent /KRAP yoo lent/ adj • Sick from drinking and/or eating too much.

Crapulent sounds so perfect for what it describes that it's hard to believe it has no connection whatsoever with *crap* or *crappy*. But it is an unrelated word with a long history, derived from the Latin *crapula* (Greek *kraipale*), meaning "drunken sickness." (*compare **bilious***)

cremaster /*krem ASS ter*/ n • One of the muscles responsible for pulling the testicles up toward the body, as in response to cold.

"With thorough and conscientious practice, Laughton had advanced from a mere dabbling in Eastern meditation all the way to **cremaster** exercises involving fishing weights."
(*compare **shram***)

creodont /*KREE o dont*/ n • A primitive small-brained animal.

Handsome suitors she had by the score,
and diamond baubles were aught that she wore.
So who could have guessed
that a woman so blessed
*would marry a **creodont** bore?*
(*compare **ephemeromorph***)

crepehanger /*KRAPE hang er*/ n • A pessimistic killjoy.

"It will probably rain," "That's not good for you," or "I saw those shoes on sale for half of what you paid." The **crepehanger** always has something deflating to say. This is a pleasingly visual word for a gloomy personality.
(*compare **marplot, snoutband***)

cresty /*KRESS tee*/ adj • Afflicted with piles (hemorrhoids).

Have you heard of people accidentally brushing their teeth with hemorrhoid ointment? It's been known to happen, but just think how much more frequently this tragic mishap would occur if there were a brand called **Cresty**.

"After his checkup, Winthorpe felt like crying: Would he

have to go through life not just short, fat, and bald, but **cresty** as well?"   (*compare **rectalgia***)

cretinize /*KREE tin ize*/ v • To cause to turn into a misshapen idiot dwarf.

It may be best to use this word metaphorically.

"Perhaps it was the gods' way of punishing her for her bad taste in having a Cinderella-themed wedding. *Something* was **cretinizing** the swashbuckling romantic Gloria had married. Now, in what were supposed to be the golden years of their marriage, he would do nothing but sit on the couch all day long, curled over a cheap beer and guffawing at reruns of Mexican wrestling."

crurotrichosis /*KREW ro trik O sis*/ n • Excessive leg hair.

"As a pop-music diva, Bettina had an image to uphold,

crurotrichosis

and her budget for personal upkeep would have maintained a fleet of ambulances. Not content with the usual retinue of hairstylist, nutritionist, manicurist, and the like, she also had a full-time staffer whose sole duty was to wage war on her chronic **crurotrichosis.**"   (*compare **pogogniasis***)

cuckquean /KUK *kween*/ n • A female cuckold; a woman whose husband is unfaithful.

Not as well-known as *cuckold,* perhaps because a woman with a cheating husband has traditionally been an object more of sympathy than scorn. It behooves us to dust off **cuckquean** and attack this blatant double standard.

(*compare **wittol***)

cully /KULL *ee*/ n • Someone who is easily imposed upon, especially by a woman.

"Julie liked to call the shots in a relationship, and she hated to be alone. But she always became bored with a man quickly, and so was always on the lookout for new prospective **cullies.**"   (*compare **dictatrix***)

cumberworld /KUM *ber world*/ n • 1) A person so deformed, lazy, or infirm as to be a burden to society. 2) A thoroughly useless person or thing.

"The culture critics argued that things had reached their all-time low, and who could disagree? Proof was the unparalleled success of the recent TV phenomenon, *Can You Be a* **Cumberworld***?,* in which contestants sat around in a sumptuously decorated apartment and each tried to be even more thoroughly useless than the others."

curpin /KUR *pin*/ n • The ass of a chicken or some other fowl.

"As she watched Kenneth greedily devour his meal of fried **curpin** in hot garlic sauce, Cynthia made a silent promise to herself that this, their first date, would also be their last."

cyesolagnia /sigh ESS o LAG nee uh/ n • The lust for pregnant women.

Proof that man is the most depraved animal in the world, for **cyesolagnia** makes no evolutionary sense at all. If there were a gene for it, wouldn't it have died out long ago? How could it be passed down, if **cyesolagniacs** waste their reproductive energy chasing after women who are already pregnant?

"Despite his family's worsening poverty, Gabriel shunned contraception, not because he wanted more children, but because of his closet **cyesolagnia**."

(*compare **gandermooner***)

cypripareunia /sip rip uh ROO nee uh/ n • Sex with a prostitute.

"Gomez knew that Mona in Accounting didn't own a dictionary, so he went ahead and included an entry for **cypripareunia** on his expense sheet."

(*compare **philopornist***)

· **D** ·

dammarel /*DAM er el*/ n • An effeminate man who spends all his time entertaining or courting women, and who is disinclined to the company of his own sex.

What a wonderfully specific word. It opens one's eyes to an entire class of men, and to the wonder that is the English language. Certainly **dammarels** must exist in other cultures, but how many tongues have a word for them?

"Woodburn the **dammarel** didn't exactly distinguish himself in The Big One. Rejected by the nursing corps and drafted into the infantry instead, he went AWOL and spent the rest of the war riveting battleships in drag."

(*compare* **badling, cotquean**)

dandilly /*dan DILL ee*/ n • A vain and spoiled woman.

Dandilly is something of a rarity, as there seem to be more words for vain males (*fop, dandy,* etc.) than for vain females in the English language. Could it be that once upon a time this vice was considered more disgraceful in a man than in a woman? And if so, why has this changed to the point where pectoral implants for men are now considered acceptable? (*compare* **muscod**)

dasypygal /*dass ip EYE gull*/ adj • Hairy-assed.

"Dr. Plimpton's heart sank when he entered his bedroom

and found his attractive young wife being mounted by Ramon, the **dasypygal** gardener."

deadhead /DED hed/ n • One who rides for free; a passenger who is not required to pay a fare.

The difference between a **deadhead** and a stowaway is that a **deadhead** does not have to hide while he siphons free rides on various conveyances. Hopefully, this excellent term will soon begin to shake loose of its musical groupie reference, and we can all go back to using **deadhead** the way it was intended.

"Bad enough that Becky's **deadhead** cousin had to cram the trunk with his guitar, forcing the other passengers to hold their bags on their laps. And that he subsisted on a type of fermented tofu, the odor of which seemed to emanate from his unwashed pores. But Justin also seemed to feel that since he wasn't contributing one penny toward gas or tolls, he was absolved from any responsibility to help fix the flat tire in the rain." (*compare* ***spunger***)

debacchate /DEB uh kate/ v • To rage in the manner of one who has drunk overmuch of liquor.

"The wedding was marred slightly by the appearance of the bride's uncle, brandishing a champagne bottle and **debacchating** that he was going to kill the man who had stolen the honor of 'his little tulip.' " (*compare* ***barlichood***)

dehorner /dee HORN er/ n • A rubbing alcohol addict.

This gem comes to us via the legal profession.

"Precisely because the congressman had subsequently committed suicide, David viewed exposing the man as a bulemic **dehorner** to be the crown jewel of his journalistic career."

dejector /dee JEK tor/ n • A drastic medicine for constipation.

"What Mrs. Ruskin didn't know was that France's quince chutney was, in fact, a **dejector** of unparalled potency—otherwise she might not have had a third helping before rushing to the airport to climb aboard the plane to Moscow." *(compare **obstipation**)*

demivierge /DEM ee vee airj/ n • A woman who is sexually promiscuous but retains her virginity.

While the authors can see nothing whatsoever that is insulting about this amazingly specific word, the definition is so delicious that we included it anyway.

To a handsome young buck named Serge
said Marge, who was feeling the urge,
"I'll give you some pleasure
but only a measure
*and remain a **demivierge**."* *(compare **hogminny**)*

desticate /DESS tik ate/ v • To cry out like a rat.

"Jonathon **desticated** in a horrid and pitiable manner, but the other boys involved in the teen prank gone awry all turned tail at the first sound of sirens, leaving him stuck halfway in the casement window." *(compare **fream**)*

diamerdis /die uh MURD iss/ n • A man who is covered in feces.

"Not only had the train ride to Paris taken sixteen hours, but Ernesto had been forced to share a small car with a subnormal **diamerdis** who insisted on sharing his cheese with him." *(compare **imbulbitate, odorivector, stinkard**)*

dictatrix /dik TAY trix/ n • A female dictator; a woman who tells people what to do.

"Exercising his own will had never been a passion for William, so he settled down with a terrible **dictatrix** named Rhonda, and soon reported that he had never been happier."

(*compare **cully***)

dietairistriae /*DIE ter ISS tree ay*/ n,pl • Women who go to female prostitutes.

Wait a second. Men who patronize ladies of the evening earn the humdrum moniker of *john,* while female customers warrant the elegant appellation of **dietairistriae?** What exactly is going on here?   (*compare **proxenetism***)

dioestrum /*die ESS trum*/ n • A period of sexual inactivity between heats.

"His friends all laughed at his credulity, but Josh believed his girlfriend whenever she told him that she was 'having a **dioestrum** at the moment.' Although he did think it somewhat odd that she always chose to fill these times by taking her car to the burly mechanic's down the road for a tune-up."

dippoldism /*DIP old ism*/ n • The spanking or whipping of young children.

This term is derived from a sadistic German schoolteacher of yore named Dippold.

"At the recently opened School for Continuing Adult Education, the course in **dippoldism** being offered for the fall semester filled up almost at once. However, when it was revealed that the school was to hire a troupe of ill-tempered midgets from the actor's union as stand-ins for the children, interest inexplicably waned."

(*compare **comprachico***)

dippoldism

disseistrix /*diss AY strix*/ n • A woman who separates someone from his or her possessions.

"The men lived in leaky houseboats and trailers off of red dirt roads. Most were alone; some had an old hound dog as a last friend from better days. They were hiding from the taxman, the lawman, and the repossessor. They were all victims of the **disseistrix,** and Josie's Roadside Tavern was the end of the line for most of them."

(*compare* **fogorner**)

dongon /*DONG on*/ n • A person who is smart but appears stupid.

"Behind the glazed eyes, the slack jaw, and the stumbling speech, there actually lay an intelligent child, but Sherwin's teachers were all fooled by the little **dongon** and had long ago chalked him up as a lost cause."

draffsack /*DRAFF sak*/ n • 1) A big paunch. 2) A lazy glutton.

Maybe this word does not possess the most exciting definitions, but it *is* insulting, and doesn't it dress up a page nicely? Originally, from a sack used to hold *draff,* meaning refuse.

"Her husband's huge **draffsack** didn't bother Mrs. Wong. She felt it lent him a certain... *substance,* and it also helped to keep other women at bay. She did wish that he wouldn't wear tight T-shirts in public quite so often, though."

(*compare* **macrogaster**)

driveler /*DRIV uh ler*/ n • One who slavers; one who talks in an idiotic fashion.

Most people are familiar with the word *drivel,* but few are aware that it exists in a form to describe an actual person. Since virtually everyone knows at least several **drivelers,** it behooves the authors to acquaint the general public with this word.

"He'd been warned that taking a bus trip across the entire country was a foolish idea at best, but Buford thought that it would be an interesting way to meet people. For two sleepless days and nights he sat scrunched next to a foul-smelling **driveler,** forced to listen to the man talk excitedly about his favorite sports biographies. Finally, he moved to the urine-soaked toilet at the back of the bus for the remainder of the trip." (*compare* **echolalia, naffin**)

dunderwhelp /DUN *der welp*/ n • A detestable numbskull.

Many people live in a fantasy world, a bubble, if you will, from which they naively view our cerebrally challenged brethren with a sort of benign acceptance. They look upon the idiots of this world as kindly folk: a bit touched perhaps, but generally good at heart. They are wrong. Stupid people are put here to make life difficult and unpleasant for the rest of us, and it is high time we described these **dunderwhelps** with the contempt they deserve.

(*compare* **knipperdollin, naffin**)

dysania /*diss AY nee uh*/ n • Difficulty getting out of bed in the morning.

There are many words in these pages that are great to use when calling in sick to work. Of these, **dysania** is the absolute best.

"I'm so sorry to miss the all-day meeting, but I'm afraid I've come down with a bad case of **dysania**." Few bosses would be cruel—or well read—enough to reject such a plaint for mercy. (*compare* **matutolagnia, ergophobia**)

dyscallignia /*diss kuh LIG nee uh*/ n • The dislike of beautiful women.

A disease that primarily afflicts women who are less than beautiful.

dyschezia /*diss KEE zee uh*/ n • Loss of the normal reflex to void the rectum, due to irregular practices.

If you're wondering what "irregular practices" are, you probably should just move on. (*compare* **megrarectum**)

dysmorphophiliac /*diss MORF o FEEL ee ak*/ n • A person with a preference for deformed sexual partners.

"It was well-known among the initiated that the ever-considerate Comtesse de Maude, consummate hostess that she was, kept a well-stocked stable of deformed sybarites, to ensure that the **dysmorphophiliacs** attending her orgies would never feel left out."   (*compare **acrotophiliac***)

dyspareunia */diss puh ROO nee uh/* n • Sex that is extremely difficult, uncomfortable, or painful.

Most people have experienced **dyspareunia** at some point in their lives. Whether it was that first time in a dark and cramped car, clumsily bumping various and sundry parts of anatomy with one's sweetheart—and becoming uncomfortably acquainted with the seat belt in the process—or the time when one's partner kept saying the wrong name.

"Too late did Jeff realize his folly in seeking to have his marriage annulled in the Texas courtroom by reason of **dyspareunia**. The preacher cum judge not only ruled against the plea, but also sternly admonished him that sex was only for the purpose of procreation, and not meant to be a pleasure."   (*compare **apophallation, psychrotic***)

ecdemolagnia /*ek dem o LAG nee uh*/ n • Extreme lustfulness when one is away from home.

Otherwise known as "marriage." (*compare* **uxoravalent**)

echolalia /*ek o LAY lee uh*/ n • Automatic and meaningless repetition of another's words and phrases.

While **echolalia** can be indicative of a mental disorder, it also crops up in people with nothing wrong with them other than that they are annoying.

"Larry's **echolalia** marked him as an imbecile. However, it also made him the perfect lackey for the schoolyard bully, and he could be seen tagging along after the ruffian all day, endlessly repeating his threats and insults. The two of them really made quite a pair." (*compare* **driveler**)

ecomaniac /*eek o MAY nee AK*/ n • One who is servile toward his boss but dictatorial toward his family.

"Simpering yes-man by day, swaggering bully by night—Sidney's **ecomania** caused him to be despised by two separate groups of people for two totally different reasons."

(*compare* **fart-sucker, subsycophant**)

edeomania /*ed ee o MAY nee uh*/ n • An obsession with genitals.

"We all enjoyed visiting the Jurgen family, especially at Christmastime, but it might have been even more enjoyable if their several large dogs hadn't been quite so **edeomaniacal** with their snouts." *(compare **lecheur**)*

effluvium /eh FLOO vee um/ n • A slight or unseen noxious vapor.

A classy word. Integral to the motto of the Wind Breaker's Club: E Pluribus **Effluvium** (Out of Many, Smelly Gas).

"Uncomfortably, the guests quietly coughed and eyed one another strangely; no one ever discovered that the subtle **effluvium** that came and went all evening had actually been the secret contribution of Snowball, the pet Persian."

*(compare **feist**)*

egrote /ee GROAT/ v • To feign sickness in order to avoid work.

Ah, to **egrote**. The question is: Is this a sin, a mark of defective character, or perhaps a sign of superior intelligence? Does the **egroter** have something that the rest of us sadly lack, and if so, how can we get it?

"Angus was always **egroting** his way out of all the unpleasant jobs at the garage. His deception finally caught up with him the day he met his demise on the oil-soaked floor, choking on a jelly doughnut as his coworkers ignored what they thought was yet another faked bout of gastrointestinal distress." *(compare **lubbard, pathodixiac**)*

eisegetical /eye zeh JET ik ul/ adj • Marked by a distorted explanation of text—especially Biblical text—to fit the meaning to preconceived notions.

"When Hazel found out that her husband had been taking the 'love thy neighbor' tenet to **eisegetical** lengths not mentioned in *her* Bible, she began spiking his coffee with a minute amount of drain clog remover each morning."

*(compare **antinomian, tartuffe**)*

elaterium /*el uh TEER ee um*/ n • The juice of the Squirting Cucumber.

A little clarification: The Squirting Cucumber (*Ecballium elaterium*) is an actual plant of the gourd family, the juice of which yields a drastic purgative. But if for reasons of delicacy you have need of a certain obscure metaphor, **elaterium** is the word for you.

"Nadia adored the tenderness with which her botany professor made love, but found it irritating when he trumpeted 'Hold me fast, dear! My **elaterium** bursts forth!'"

*(compare **dejector**)*

elumbated /*el UM bay ted*/ adj • Weak in the loins.

This word describes the unhappy state of certain older men who take much younger wives and subsequently become **elumbated** from the constant pressure to perform in bed. Typical symptoms include: dark, liverish circles under the eyes, the paying of undue attention to diet and exercise, and the spending of hour upon hour desperately combing through Chinatown apothecaries in search of vitalizing herbal tonics.

"Dewey cursed himself for his incessant and chronic masturbation: offered a chance to score with a real-live girl, he'd been far too **elumbated** to perform."

*(compare **pudendagra**)*

emetomaniac /*em ET o MAY nee ak*/ n • A person with an abnormal propensity to vomit frequently.

"With their bold promises and flashy advertising campaign ('Eat like a cow and still lose weight!!!'), the authors of *The Ruminant's Cookbook* made a fortune by tapping into a lucrative and largely unexplored vein of **emetomania** in the general public."   (*compare **bevomit, hyperemian***)

empleomaniac /*em PLEE o MAY nee ak*/ n • One who is overly eager to hold public office.

People who are overeager to hold public office obviously fall into one of three categories: 1) They are inherently corrupt and seek to make a fortune at the taxpayer's expense. 2) They are simpleminded or delusional enough to believe that they can actually "make a difference." 3) They are completely insane.

It doesn't matter which category they fall into; **empleomaniacs** should be immediately disqualified for any public office higher than school crossing guard.

(*compare **malversation***)

encopresis /*EN ko PREE sis*/ n • Inability to control the bowels.

Here is a word that literally means to lose one's shit. Best used in sentences like the following:

"Mr. and Mrs. Spatchcock nearly had **encopresis** when they returned from their trip abroad and found that a troupe of carrot-farming squatters had laid claim to their lawn."   (*compare **copracrasia***)

engrease /*en GREASE*/ v • To become fat.

"Gus loved being a short-order cook. The pop and sizzle of frying bacon, the buzz of hungry customers. Sadly, as a result of his thrifty yet ill-advised habit of ending each shift by eating all the griddle scraps with a side helping of liquid lard, he was **engreasing** at an alarming rate."

(*compare **lipophilic***)

entheomaniac /*en THEE o MAY nee ak*/ n • One who is literally insane about religion.

"Easter seemed to lose some of its carefree spirit for the children the year they celebrated it at the country home of their Aunt Helen, an **entheomaniac** who insisted that they recite an hour of the Scriptures before hunting for eggs. She ended the day with a lecture on what happens to children who go to Hell, illustrated nicely by microwaving a foil-wrapped chocolate bunny rabbit."   (*compare **tartuffe***)

enuresis /*en yoo REE sis*/ n • Bed-wetting.

"Jefferey's parents just couldn't bring themselves to wean their little darling off diapers at a respectable age—leaving him with a lifelong case of **enuresis**."   (*compare **nocturia***)

ephemeromorph /*ef EM er o morf*/ n • Term used to describe the lowest forms of life imaginable, so low they cannot be otherwise classified.

Evade classification though they might, **ephemeromorphs** can easily be recognized. They are usually seen blocking intersections in their cars, or, in the subway, clipping their nails while taking up three seats.   (*compare **creodont***)

epicaricacy /*ep ik AAH rik uh see*/ n • Pleasure from the misfortunes of others.

An underutilized jewel. What a word! What a concept! It should bring joy to the hearts of all the people (the majority of the readers of this volume) who chuckle inwardly when they see someone trip and fall or step into a glistening pile of dog droppings.

Sadly, **epicaricacy** has been unfairly neglected over the years. Numerous modern English dictionaries make no mention of it; meanwhile, they see fit to include the German word *schadenfreude* (same definition), apparently for the sole reason that it fills a void in our language! The fact is, long before *schadenfreude* wormed its way into the lexicon, there existed an English word for the exact same concept. **Epicaricacy** has a noble lineage, coming from the Greek roots of *epi* (upon) + *chara* (joy) + *kakon* (evil). And it has appeared in many old and esteemed dictionaries. Yet the word is now largely ignored in favor of a foreign interloper.

"The residents of quiet, tree-lined Bowker Street were a peaceful lot as a rule, but their feathers got a bit ruffled when the local ice cream truck man refused to lower the volume of the horrid wheedling music his vehicle constantly emanated. And so when the deranged war veteran from the next block destroyed the truck with a bazooka one fine spring morning, they all felt the warm glow of **epicaricacy** spreading through their veins."

*(compare **ucalegon**)*

epigone */ep IG uh nee/* n • 1) An imitator born in a later generation. 2) An undistinguished follower of an accomplished master.

This can be a useful word and it makes an excellent underhanded insult. **Epigones** abound in many fields: the arts are one clear example. And so few people grasp the true meaning of this word, especially when slipped into everyday conversation, that if a candidate for higher office were to be introduced to the masses as "the **epigone** of a long line of American patriots," he would probably not lose many votes.

epigynum /ep ih JINE um/ n • The vagina of a spider.

"With the prospect of **epigynum** luring him forward, Max, the male black widow spider, ignored the obvious danger and advanced into the web."

eproctolagniac /eh PROK toe LAG nee ak/ n • Someone who is sexually stimulated by flatulence, his own or someone else's.

Some men keep a porn collection under their bed for those occasions when they desire to be intimate with themselves. For the **eproctolagniac,** a jar of refried beans is more effective.   (*compare **aerocolpos, feist***)

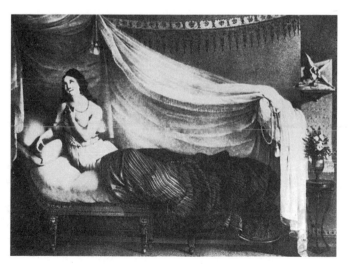

eproctolagniac

ergophobia /ERG o FO bee uh/ n • Hatred or fear of work.

Because phobias are boring, dime-a-dozen affairs, only a few are included in this book. **Ergophobia** is one of them. A word so useful should be brought to people's attention, phobia though it may be. (*compare* **dysania**)

erotomania /eh ROTE o MAY nee uh/ n • Obsessive, uncontrollable craving for sex.

"Jacobson's **erotomania** had led him down many dark and dangerous paths before, but now, as he faced the mob of enraged harpies, he realized for the first time that he needed help." (*compare* **lascivia, tentigo, satyriasis**)

eructation /eh ruk TAY shun/ n • A belching; also, the gas brought up by belching.

"Allan picked up the telephone receiver and winced; a waft of the last person's **eructations** still lingered in the mouthpiece." (*compare* **fumosities, nidorosities**)

eviration /eh vir AY shun/ n • Effeminization; the assumption of female mannerisms by a man.

"It certainly was disconcerting to see a big, strong lumberjack like Rusty undergo a complete **eviration** in the infirmary, all because of one little splinter." (*compare* **badling, cotquean, dammarel**)

excerebrose /ex SEH reh brose/ adj • Brainless.

This word not only describes the Scarecrow from *The Wizard of Oz*, but a significant portion of humanity as well—and certainly the bulk of our cultural output. Do not confuse **excerebrose** with the remarkably similar *ex-*

cerebrate (to beat the brains out), although the one might very well prompt the other.

"As a producer, Rutman skyrocketed to moguldom behind a series of lowbrow comedies starring a lovable chimpanzee, each film being more **excerebrose** than the last."

*(compare **dunderwhelp**)*

exopthalmos */ex op THAL mose/* adj • Having protruding eyeballs; bug-eyed.

"Jerry, the hypertensive and **exopthalmos** middle manager who always needed things done yesterday, trod all over the secretarial pool for years. When he finally suffered a massive heart attack while trying to unjam the copy machine, all the ladies chipped in and purchased a large gilt frame to enshrine the offending piece of crinkled paper."

*(compare **blattoid**)*

expeditate */ex PED it ate/* v • To hobble a dog by cutting out the balls of its feet.

Formerly practiced to keep dogs from chasing deer.

*(compare **hamble**)*

exsibilate */ex SIB il ate/* v • To hiss off the stage.

For all the drama buffs out there: the only word that one really needs to know when discussing bad theater.

*(compare **cantabank**)*

eyeservant */EYE serv ent/* n • One who works only when being watched.

Everyone has a little bit of **eyeservant** in them. Face it: The only thing that keeps most of us working at our jobs is the fear of being found out if we don't. Those who can coast, do.

"Starting and stopping so many times took almost as much energy as working the whole day through, but Wilson was a proud and practiced **eyeservant,** gifted with astounding peripheral vision, and without a foreman looking in his direction, he wouldn't dig."

(compare aidle, ploiter)

fabiform /FAB *if orm*/ adj • Shaped like a bean.

Fabiform cuts to the quick of what this book is all about: providing the most specific and exact term to correctly insult every person one might possibly encounter. No matter how well versed one is in the art of vulgarity, one can always use a word that will slice through a target's defenses, precisely summing up their flaws to the extent that they feel truly horrible about themselves. **Fabiform** is such a word.

Granted, "shaped like a bean" is not a concept that immediately evokes images of grown men breaking down and crying upon hearing themselves thus described. But if one takes a moment to picture in one's mind a kidney bean, with its distinctive curvature, and then adds a set of arms, legs, and a head to it, an image coalesces of a swaybacked sort of man, his stomach protruding a full twelve inches in front of where his skinny shoulders are: a **fabiform** man.

(*compare* **pyriform**)

fadge /FAJ/ n • A clumsy oaf.

"From the vantage point of a comfortable middle age, Mr. Johnstone looked back fondly on his public-school days, especially the crisp autumn mornings when he and his mates would torture and humiliate the class **fadge**, often reducing the poor boy to tears." (*compare* **looby**)

fanaticise /fan AT iss ize/ v • To behave like a fanatic.

Fanatic is a common word for an all-too-common type of individual. But most people are unaware that it exists as a verb as well.

"Luther **fanaticised** over his diet and the diets of those around him incessantly, straining his leafy green vegetables every night before going to bed and constantly upbraiding his roommates over their caloric intake. One day when they could take no more, they tied him to a chair and force-fed him pickled herring until he wept."

(*compare* **knipperdollin**)

fart-sucker /FART suk er/ n • A brown-noser; one who sucks up to superiors.

"Pettiford didn't mind running errands for his boss; it was a sure-fire way to climb the corporate ladder. And while it also didn't bother him when he became known within the firm as 'the little **fart-sucker,**' he did wish his coworkers would at least stick to his official title in company memos."   (*compare* **ecomaniac, subsycophant**)

feague /FEEG/ v • To insert an energizing suppository into the anus of a horse, in order to make it sprightly and to perk up its tail.

Feague has had a wide variety of meanings over the centuries, from "a dull, lazy oaf" to "to whip or thrash someone." The only definition that interests us, however, concerns the anus of a horse.

In times gone by, **feaguing** was commonly employed to "pep up" horses being shown for sale. A good **feague** could consist of one of several things, the most common being a suppository of raw ginger. In a pinch (or if stronger measures were called for, as in the case of a particularly

feague

sluggish or decrepit nag), owners sometimes resorted to the insertion of a live eel.

It is hard to imagine a less enviable job than that of *feaguer.*

Interestingly, **feague** was at one time used in a figurative sense, to mean to encourage or lift the spirits of a person.

(*compare* **trocar**)

fecaloid /*FEEK uh loid*/ adj • Resembling dung.

Now, instead of expressing your displeasure by calling something shitty, or saying that it looks, smells, or sounds like shit, you may damn it as **fecaloid.**

"And so off we went, to yet another blistering Fourth of July picnic, where I would be obliged to eat several of my father-in-law's burnt and **fecaloid** hamburgers while enduring his inane chatter."

(*compare* **ordurous, stercoraceous, urinous**)

feculent /FEK yoo lent/ adj • Covered in feces.

The world would probably be a happier place if we never had need for a word like **feculent**. Unfortunately, situations calling for its use are more common than one might at first believe. It might even have a place in negative restaurant reviews—used metaphorically, of course.

"Trying out his new Rollerblades for the first time, Fullerton brought his mastiff down to the overused dog run in the park after a rainstorm. He was so horridly **feculent** when he finally made it back home that his doorman wouldn't let him into the building without first hosing him off on the sidewalk."

*(compare **bedung, diamerdis**)*

feist /FEIST/ n • A silent fart.

Why is this word not included in dictionaries of today? It is a major instance of modern lexicography gone awry. **Feist** is exactly the sort of word that would prick up the ears of any thirteen-year-old, doing wonders to spark a more-than-superficial interest in our language. Perhaps *that's* why....

"The disgusting and flatulent little toad from Word Processing was forever in the habit of letting loose with **feists** while lunching in the company cafeteria, and would always give himself away by tittering loudly when he did so."

*(compare **eproctolagniac**)*

fenks /FENX/ n, pl • Discarded whale blubber, once used for manuring.

"The docks were often a dangerous place for a landlubber, so scattered were they with slippery **fenks**."

*(compare **flense**)*

ferule /FEH rull/ v • To punish schoolchildren by striking them on the hands with a **ferule** (a short stick or ruler).

"Mr. Peabody, the headmaster, had always been a zealous advocate of the **ferule**; after the school ended its use, he quietly took to drink."

(compare **bastinado, pandy**)

fico /FIKE o/ n • A gesture, thrusting the thumb between the middle and forefinger of a closed fist, that is indicative of deep contempt.

While this word is not terribly insulting in and of itself, it does have a romantic and insulting pedigree.

Let us go back in time to strife-torn twelfth-century Europe. Our story centers on Frederick Barbarossa, a German prince who captured Milan in the 1160s, but was expelled a short time later. While removing him from their city, the Milanese took occasion to humiliate Barbarossa's wife in a manner unspecified by accounts of the period. He was not a man to look kindly upon such a deed (whatever it was), so when he retook Milan he exacted a strange and horrific revenge.

He began by having every able-bodied man of the city kneel behind the posterior of a defecating mule. As the mule voided what he had to void, the poor man behind it was forced, on pain of death, to take the lump of excrement between his teeth and, turning to his captors, say, "Ecco la fica" ("Behold the fig").

Although the physical gesture in question has been around since time immemorial, only after Freddy Barbarossa did it assume the meaning that it has today. He truly was the father of the **fico**, and in this respect he was a visionary.

fimiculous /fim IK yoo luss/ adj • Dwelling in dung; existing on excrement.

"Sleeping in the barn was a step up in life for Gruber, the **fimiculous** manure boy." *(compare **shardborn**)*

fireship /FIRE ship/ n • A diseased prostitute.

A very special and very troubling word. While we are by no means seeking to cast judgment on prostitution (patrons or purveyors), a diseased prostitute is a fairly unappetizing notion by any measure.

" 'Boss Fats' McKenzie was no do-gooder, and preferred to be a hands-off mayor, but when the spread of **fireships** threatened his town's lucrative prostitution trade, he leapt into action quicker than the Sisters of Mercy at a church picnic struck by lightning." *(compare **frenchified**)*

fissilingual /FISS il ING wool/ adj • Possessing a forked tongue.

"Staring out at his barren window box, Boddington cursed that **fissilingual** convenience-store owner. He should never have agreed to trade his winning lottery ticket for a pouch of 'magic beans.' " *(compare **abydocomist**)*

flagellant /FLAJ uh lent/ n • A sexual deviant who enjoys beating or being beaten.

"A serious **flagellant,** Rufus would twice weekly immerse his entire body in a tub of cold cream in order to render himself all the more sensitive to the delicious taste of the whip." *(compare **algolagnia**)*

flatus /FLAT us/ n • Gas in the stomach or intestines. Also, gas expelled from the anus.

flagellant

This word, from the Latin for "a blowing," is one technical term for a fart.

(*compare* **bdolotic, carminative, meteorism**)

fleam /FLEEM/ n • A hollow lancet formerly used by surgeons to pierce the flesh and draw blood.

"Maybe it was just too far ahead of its time, but Doctor Barber's **fleam**-exchange program never quite caught on."

(*compare* **bdellatomy**)

flense /FLENZ/ v • To strip the blubber off an animal such as a whale.

"Diets were useless, exercise out of the question: nothing

fleam

outside of a drastic **flensing** could help Otto, the human medicine ball." *(compare fenks)*

fogorner /FOG *or ner*/ n • Formerly, a person whose job it was to expel people from their residences.

"Patsy just loved working as a **fogorner.** The shocked looks on the families' faces when she served the eviction notices, the wails and piteous cries of the indignant, and most of all, the feeling that she was really accomplishing something. Why, it made her feel all proud inside."

(compare disseistrix)

foveated /FO *vee ate ed*/ adj • Covered with little pits, such as those left from smallpox.

Apart from golf balls and English muffins, few things improve from being **foveated.**

"Bad enough that Wayne had broken out in a terrible case of acne on the eve of the prom, but his do-it-yourself remedy with household bleach and a turkey baster left his face more **foveated** than a brick of baby Swiss cheese."

(*compare **plooky***)

franion /FRAN *yun*/ n • A man of loose behavior; a pleasure seeker.

It is one of the gross inequalities of the English language that while there are literally dozens of words to describe women of promiscuous behavior, words for their male counterparts are exceedingly scarce. So make the most of **franion**.

(*compare **cicisbeo***)

fream /FREEM/ v • To roar like a wild boar during the rutting season, when he seeks to mate.

"Douglaston continued his nightly ritual of adding to an already porcine physique with a diet of low-grade beer and stale bar pretzels. And although he was practically **freaming** at every woman who entered the bar, not one of them ever showed the slightest inclination to go outside and rut with him in his minivan."

(*compare **strene***)

frenchified /FRENCH *if ide*/ adj • 1) To have contracted a venereal disease. 2) To have become like the French.

Most people are aware of the second definition of this adjective, but not the first (although it is a toss-up as to which of the twain is more insulting). One must really give credit for this word where credit is due; namely to the English and their peculiar blend of humor, disdain, and good old-fashioned xenophobia.

"Lisa Hickstrom's parents breathed a sigh of relief. The news sounded good: Their formerly wayward teen daughter was becoming 'thoroughly **frenchified**' in Paris on the study-abroad program. Apparently a change of scenery was just what the young hellion needed."

*(compare **fireship**, **ranivorous**)*

fricatrice /FRIK *uh triss*/ n • A harlot; a lewd woman. Also, a lesbian; a female genital rubber.

Were it not for its secondary meaning, **fricatrice,** like countless other English words for women of dubious morals—including (to name a few) *gig, giglet, callet, co-cotte, blowen, drassock, dratchel, drotchel, drazel, doxy, cyprian, leman, leveret, mab, puttock, rep, demirep, slat-tern, slaister, ploot, jade, demimondaine, meretrix, harlot, strumpet,* and *quean*—would not have made it into this book. *(compare **tribade**)*

frottage /FROT *ij*/ n • The practice of rubbing up against another person while clothed, in the pursuit of sexual satisfaction.

Isn't it comforting to know that the next time you're on a city bus and someone presses his groin against your butt, you will have a word for it?

frotteur /*fro* TIRRH/ n • A man who performs **frottage.** A female **frotteur** is known as a *frotteuse.*

fubsy /FUB *zee*/ adj • Plump and squat.

There are many, many words to describe short and fat people in the English language. Most of them, for reasons that remain unclear, are of Scottish origin, and the over-whelming majority of them are very dull indeed. Since it is unlikely that you will ever come across the need for more than one of these words, the authors give you **fubsy.**

"Behind six months in his rent, Nestor heard the pounding at his door and ran to the back exit, only to be intercepted by his **fubsy**, rolling-pin-wielding landlady."

(*compare* **smatchet**)

fumosities /few MOSS it eez/ n • Ill-smelling vapors from a drunken person's belches.

"'How did you know the defendant was under the influence?' the judge asked the testifying officer. 'I smelled his **fumosities**, sir,' he replied."

(*compare* **eructation, nidorosities**)

furfuraceous /FUR fur AY shuss/ adj • Covered in dandruff; afflicted with dandruff.

"Young Jennifer had just moved to the big city from the suburbs, and so much wanted to become one of the 'in' crowd that she would always dress completely in black. The problem was, she was so **furfuraceous** that she had to discreetly carry a little whisk brush with her at all times."

fussock /FUSS uk/ n • A large, fat woman.

A good word to use, for instance, for the lady ahead of you in line who accidentally stomps on your foot with her ridiculously tiny heels.

"Eventually Wilbur's passion overcame him, and he plunged into the **fussock** like a squirrel into a pile of leaves."

(*compare* **fustilugs**)

fustigate /FUSS tig ate/ v • To beat with a stick or club.

A hearty, meaty word. Sometimes it is a good idea to relax, sit back, and think of all the people you would like

fussock

to see **fustigated**. From the Latin *fustis* (club), *fustuarium* (execution by clubbing), and *fustigare* (to cudgel to death).

(*compare* **urticate**)

fustilarian /FYOOST il AIR ee an/ n • One who pursues worthless objects or aims.

That this word describes almost all of us is one bleak observation. Not to be preachy, but **fustilarian** certainly provides food for thought, because what a person sees as worthless depends on what a person values: A greedy fellow who only cares for money might consider someone who pursues love to be a **fustilarian**.

(*compare **nihilarian***)

fustilugs /*FUSS tee lugs*/ n • An unwieldy and slovenly woman.

"Life as a circus fat lady was no walk in the park, Edelle the **fustilugs** realized. Despite her immense girth, she was expected to trot around the entire ring thrice daily."

(*compare **fussock***)

fustigate

· G ·

gambrinous /GAM *brin us*/ adj • Full of beer.

"Helmut was never able to leave a soiree until he was properly **gambrinous,** and usually suffered horribly the next morning as a result."   (*compare **potvaliant***)

gammerstang /GAM *er stang*/ n • A tall, skinny, and awkward woman.

"Who could have predicted that the shy young **gammerstang,** forever bumping her head on doorways and blushing in company, would blossom into a gorgeous and successful runway model? Or that she would soon metamorphose again, this time into a pill-popping, anorexic prima donna?"   (*compare **scrag***)

gamomania /gam o MAY *nee uh*/ n • Insanity characterized by the compulsion to make outlandish marriage proposals.

"In order to avoid an extremely expensive settlement with his estranged wife, Benson embraced an unusual legal strategy: annullment by reason of **gamomania.**"

(*compare **hypobulia, mariturient***)

ganch /GANCH/ v • To execute by impaling upon hooks or stakes.

Victims of this delightful practice were often tossed from

a platform onto the aforementioned hooks and stakes. Even today, careless casting can result in by-standers being **ganched** on the fishing pier.

"After an exquisite meal, guests retired to the salon for snifters of cognac, where Bishop Montleby's suggestion that **ganching** be reinstated for debtors was met with hearty approval from all assembled."

gandermooner /GAND er moon er/ n • A man who chases women during the month after his wife has given birth.

This is an amazingly specific word. A **gandermooner** is not just a man who cheats on his wife, but one who cheats on his wife during a very narrow window of opportunity. It raises a question: When was this phenomenon so pronounced as to have warranted a special term?

"Some of the regulars in the pub liked to reminisce about their honeymoons, but not old Mr. McGillicuddy. The old **gandermooner's** chief source of delight lay in reliving the many escapades he had enjoyed as the father of twelve—and in cursing his twins for 'cheating' him out of yet another one." *(compare liffy)*

gardyloo /gar dee LOO/ exclamation • Formerly, a cry given just prior to throwing household slops or the contents of one's chamber pot out the window, warning those on the street below. *(compare bemute)*

gaucy /GOSS ee/ adj • Fat and comely.

Note that a person so described is unlikely to overflow with gratitude. Half insult and half compliment, **gaucy** is useful when one wishes to deprecate someone in the nicest way possible.

This girl I once knew was the heights—
nay, the acme of fleshy delights.
*Sweet-faced and **gaucy**,*
my trollop so saucy,
I miss her on cold winter nights.

(compare cacocallia)

gavage /*guv AHZH*/ n • The force-feeding of geese or other fowl to fatten them or enlarge their livers. Also, any force-feeding.

" 'What goes around comes around,' thought Wendy at Christmas dinner, as her grandmother piled more of the burnt goose—probably a victim of **gavage** itself—onto her plate." *(compare **impinguinate**)*

genicon /*JEN ik on*/ n • An imagined sexual partner visualized during sex, in order to facilitate pleasure.

(The imagined partner can be real, just not present at the time.)

"Sonya eventually grew tired of trying to force herself to be attracted to her husband, and relied more and more upon her **genicons** for fulfillment." *(compare **allorgasmia**)*

geromorphism /*jeh ro MORF ism*/ n • The condition of appearing older than one's age.

"In a state of total denial, Penny refused to even consider that her daily tanning sessions might have something to do with her advanced **geromorphism**."

geromorphic /*jer o MORF ik*/ adj • Prematurely aged; appearing older than one is.

In today's youth-obsessed culture, being **geromorphic** is a fate worse than death. But as strange as it may sound, in certain long-forgotten periods of history old people were actually respected and admired. At those times, **geomorphism** had a silver lining, as it does today for underage drinkers.

"At first Liz's new classmates shunned the unlucky girl with the lined, leathery skin and graying hair. But after she demonstrated her ability to put her **geromorphism** to good use procuring wine coolers, she became very popular on Friday and Saturday nights." *(compare raddled)*

gerontophilia /*jeh ront uh FEEL ee uh*/ n • Sexual attraction to elderly men.

"No lecher was he—merely another victim of the latest sexual fad of bored and hip young women: **gerontophilia**." *(compare anililagnia)*

giddhom /*GID hum*/ n • The frantic galloping of cows plagued by flies.

Giddhom is such an amusing and potentially useful word—why not extend its meaning to cover, say, human beings on camping trips?

"Three nights and two days of hell and Dylan snapped; unfortunately, his half-mad **giddhom** only had the effect of attracting thicker clouds of mosquitoes."

gink /*GINK*/ n • An insignificant person.

"At their tenth high school reunion, all of the former cheerleaders and football players were quietly outraged that the class **gink,** whom almost no one remembered at all, had gone on to become a computer mogul of enormous wealth. At their twentieth reunion, they were all secretly pleased with the news that he had died of an aneurysm the previous spring."

gleet /GLEET/ n • In ascending order of vileness:
1. any slimy and viscous substance
2. a persistent sinus inflammation
3. a thick phlegm found in the stomachs of hawks
4. thin, milky urethral discharge
5. runoff from a gonorrheal sore

glouping /GLAU ping/ adj • Dumb and sullen.

The word **glouping** somehow just *looks* dumb and sullen. Anyone who has been on a rainy camping trip with young children should be familiar with its meaning.

glump /GLUMP/ n • A sulking crank.

"Old Mr. Kemp truly hated children, and cultivated his reputation as the town **glump** by sitting on a park bench all day long, spitting bits and pieces of wet popcorn at the mothers who passed by with their strollers."

gobbets /GOB its/ n, pl • Pieces of human bodies that wash ashore from a shipwreck.

Gobbet, a generic word for a lump of flesh, is more familiar to most people than **gobbets**, which is remarkable for its gruesome specificity.   (*compare* **adipocere**)

gobemouche /go beh MOOSH/ n • A gullible person.

Deriving from the French (literally "swallow-fly"; i.e., one who will swallow anything), **gobemouche** is a nice, memorable little term for a credulous person.

"The sweepstakes people had unearthed a true **gobemouche** in Cassandra. Every time she got a piece of junk mail telling her she had 'already won a million dollars,' she hopped on a plane and flew down to their headquarters to pick up her nonexistent winnings."

glouping

goller /GOLL *er*/ v • To utter loud and unintelligible gurgling noises, especially when shouting in rage.

This happens rather frequently with enraged people and is usually quite funny to watch—from a distance. What red-blooded child doesn't enjoy provoking a substitute teacher or some other adult victim to the point where he or she starts to **goller**?

"As Glanders watched his new seventy-five-foot yacht

being bashed to and fro in the marina with his idiot son-in-law at the controls, he could do nothing but stand at the end of the dock, **gollering** in impotent fury."

(compare agrammaticist)

gongoozler /gon GOOZ ler/ n • A dimwit who stares at unusual things.

The term **gongoozler** was formerly applied to a type of lowlife who hung out of windows and gaped at passersby. In certain neighborhoods this creature is still alive and well today. However, the authors suggest extending the word to include, say, people who stare out of the windows of automobiles. Imagine the traffic reporter saying, "We have fifteen-minute delays on the George Washington Bridge, where traffic is all backed up due to a three-car accident and **gongoozling** in the left lane...."

gound /GOWND/ n • The crusty yellow substance that collects in the corners of one's eyes while one sleeps.

Everybody gets this stuff in the corners of their eyes while they sleep, and nobody really knows what to call it. Typical terms invented to fill this vacuum include *sleepies, eye-snot,* and *bed-boogers.* The correct word, however, is **gound.**

"Collin was never one to dillydally in the morning: by the time he had rubbed the **gound** out of his eyes he was usually on his third Manhattan." (*compare* **ceruminosis**)

graveolent /gruh VAY o lent/ adj • Having an offensive and fetid odor.

There are so many horrible smells in the world. In fact, fifty new ones are invented every day. New words to describe them, therefore, should be welcomed by all.

(compare stinkard)

grimalkin /grim ALL kin/ n • A jealous or imperious old woman.

[*gray* + *malkin* mop, scarecrow, kitchen maid, or cat]

Grimalkin is a pretty nasty word to call a woman, perfect for occasions that call for the strongest form of verbal abuse.

"Cindy knew the spiteful old **grimalkins** on the parole board would never have mercy on *her*—a young and gorgeous game-show hostess who had it all but got mixed up in the dangerous world of tropical-fish smuggling. She concentrated instead on plans for escape." (*compare beldam*)

grimthorpe /GRIM thorp/ v • To do a rotten job of restoration.

So called after Sir Edmund Beckett, the first Baron Grimthorpe, an architect who was severely criticized for his botched restoration of St. Albans Cathedral in England.

"When the refuse from the toilet began flowing from the kitchen faucets, it became clear to us that our house had been **grimthorped** in the worst possible way."

(*compare antivitruvian*)

grizely /GRIZ uh lee/ adj • Extraordinarily ugly.

Thanks in large part to modern architecture, new words for "extremely ugly" are always in demand. And while saying that something "looks like shit" will always get the point across, the reader may find it marginally empowering to have **grizely** at his disposal, even if he would really prefer a wrecking ball.

"Dominick, the high-strung and aesthetically snobbish interior decorator, recoiled in horror from his community service assignment. For shoplifting designer scarves, he was sentenced to helping seniors craft **grizely** mobiles out of shrinky-dinks and dried macaroni; he wished he'd been sentenced to jail instead." *(compare **igly**)*

groak /GROAK/ v • To stare silently at someone while they are eating, in the hope that they will offer some food.

Groak is one of the finest all-around words in this book. It is fun to say, easy to remember, and somehow manages to sound like what it means, even though what it describes is a silent action. And the definition, while not as depraved as some other words, is both amusing and instantly applicable in life.

"Flowers, reservations for two at the best restaurant in town: Trevor's date was going exactly as planned—except for the pair of **groaking** hobos with their noses pressed right up against the glass." *(compare **scrambler**)*

gubbertush /GUB er tush/ n • A bucktoothed person.

"Once a year for an entire week in August the townspeople would line up and cheer on Belvedere, the scrawny, tow-headed little **gubbertush**, as he defeated all comers in the county-wide corn-eating contest. Effortlessly sawing row after row of kernels into his mouth, for those few days he was their hometown pride." *(compare **brochity**)*

gugusse /guh GOOSE/ n • A young homosexual with a penchant for priests.

"The cardinal sought out a plump young **gugusse** for himself, but had to settle for a slightly unwilling altarboy." *(compare **gunsel**)*

gulchin /GULL chin/ n • A little or young glutton.

"It was always good sport to tease and steal the lunch of Harvey, the rotund **gulchin** in the fourth grade, but it was almost too easy. He wept at the drop of a hat, and besides, he was far too portly to chase anybody very far."

(*compare* **barathrum**)

gundygut /*GUN dee gut*/ n • An offensive, mannerless eater.

This is a fine term of somewhat jocular abuse, good among other things for hammering home table manners to small children: "Take human bites, you **gundyguts!**"

"Whenever Sheryl wanted to shed a couple of pounds, she would wait until twelve o'clock and peer over the cubicle wall at her coworker with the muttonchop sideburns. Watching that **gundygut** stuff his face invariably put her off her lunch."

(*compare* **slotterhodge**)

gunsel /*GUN zul*/ n • The orally passive member of a male homosexual union. Also, a gunman.

A word with an unusual history. It entered the English language from the German *gänslein* (little goose) and originally meant a passive male lover. But in 1929, Dashiell Hamett slyly inserted it into his famous novel *The Maltese Falcon* in reference to a young homosexual gunman. Since many people at the time seemed ignorant of the fact that two men could be lovers, **gunsel** was read by most as a simple synonym for "gunman." This secondary meaning has since remained in the language.

(*compare* **gugusse, irrumate**)

gurry /*GIRRH ee*/ n • Medical waste from dissecting rooms. Also, refuse from fishing and whaling.

"Chip knew it was a demanding way to work his way through medical school, but bagging up the **gurry** happened to be one of the highest-paying jobs on campus."

(*compare* **fenks**)

gynander /*guy NAN der*/ n • A mannish woman.

"In a last-ditch effort to elude his homosexual tendencies, Cromwell married a young **gynander** who came equipped with both a vile temper and a significant moustache." (*compare **viraginity***)

gynecomast /*GUY nek o mast*/ n • A man suffering from **gynecomastia** (outsized, flaccid, feminine breasts).

gynecomastia / *guy nek o MAST ee uh*/ n • A condition whereby a man's breasts swell to abnormal size, coming to resemble those of a woman in appearance and/or function.

"Raymond eschewed doctors, and working with a homemade surgical kit of knitting needles, rubber plugs, and Super Glue, bravely dealt with his **gynecomastia** on his own." (*compare **androgalactozemia***)

gynopiper /*GUY no pipe er*/ n • One who stares lewdly at women.

One of the beautiful things about **gynopiper** is that, like its cousin **arrhenopiper**, it does not specify the sex of the person doing the ogling. (*compare **arrhenopiper***)

· H ·

hamble /*HAM bull*/ v • To cripple a dog by cutting out the balls of its feet.

"Jefferson, the unbalanced mailman, finally snapped one day: his arrest for criminal assault with intent to **hamble** a cocker spaniel made the evening news."

*(compare **expeditate**)*

hamesucken /*HAME suk en*/ n • Felonious assault of someone in his own home.

Go on, laugh! It's *funny!*

hemothymia /*hee mo THIGH mee uh*/ n • The irresistable desire to murder.

"When her husband announced that he was leaving her for a woman named Kiki twenty years her junior, Doris felt the **hemothymia** begin to swell within her."

*(compare **jugulate**)*

hippomanic /*hip o MAN ik*/ adj • Lusting after horses.

"Geoffrey Vanderbern was the most renowned polo player in the district, due largely to the uncanny rapport he shared with Platypus, his faithful mount. When a meddling scandalmonger threatened to expose him as a **hippomanic**

hemothymia

deviant, it cost him two of his country houses to have the
story quashed."   (*compare **avisodomy***)

hircine */HER sine/* adj • Smelling like a goat.
  "Had he been a tad less **hircine**, I might actually have
enjoyed my afternoon sessions with the venerable Mon-
signor Wilby."   (*compare **caprylic, rammish***)

hircismus */her SIZ muss/* n • A malodorous condition of
the armpits.
  "So worried was Prufrock about his **hircismus** that prior
to his big date he wrapped his armpits entirely with duct
tape."   (*compare **maschalephidrosis***)

hirquiticke */her KWIT ik/* n • "One past foureteene yeeres
of age, beginning to bee moved with venus delight" (Cockeram's *English Dictionarie* of 1623).

Most people look back on this tender and vulnerable stage of awakening sexuality with a certain nostalgia, tempered by an overwhelming relief that they never have to go through it again. (*compare **demivierge***)

hogminny /*hog MIN ee*/ n • A depraved young woman.

Just like beauty, that which is insulting is entirely in the eye of the beholder.

"Nursing their hot toddies on cold autumn nights, the lads in the tavern loved to hoist their robust voices in song. And none of their ditties ever brought more tears to more eyes than that wistful ode, *Winnie My **Hogminny**.*"

(*compare **parepithymia***)

hogminny

huskanoy /HUSK *uh noy*/ v • To subject to repeated enemas, especially as a form of initiation.

"At the press conference, the dean emphatically defended the fraternities that had come under fire for hazing: 'So what if a few of the lads have been getting **huskanoyed** here and there,' he said, 'where's the harm in that?'"

(*compare* **clyster**)

hybristophiliac /hib RIST o FEEL ee ak/ n • One who becomes sexually aroused from being with a violent criminal.

In spite of the inherent danger involved (or perhaps because of it), **hybristophiliacs** are doing their part to ensure that the Evil Gene gets passed down to the next generation.

"Dedicated to discreetly servicing **hybristophiliac** women with means, www.dateafelon.com quickly grew from a small Internet start-up into a cyber cash cow."

(*compare* **kleptolagnia**)

hygeiolatry /hi jee OLL uh tree/ n • Health fanaticism.

This word is more useful today than ever, for even as the population as a whole grows more obese and sickly, a lunatic fringe errs in the other direction. These odd and pathetic creatures are easily identified not by their aversion to steak, cheese, and all the other things that generally make life worth living, but by their hysterical opposition to anyone who seems to be enjoying himself.

"The frequent ice-cold plunge baths, the rolfings, the all-squid diet...it was all part and parcel of Marlon's **hygeiolatry**—as were the sunken cheeks, the greenish complexion, and the disagreeable body odor."

(*compare* **fanaticise, knipperdollin**)

hypereccrisia /hi per ek RIZH ee uh/ n • An abnormal amount of excretion.

If the sheer quantity of what lies in the bowl defies the senses and makes you worry about the capacity of your household plumbing, then you are truly suffering from **hypereccrisia**.

"When her little brother yelled from the bathroom for her to 'come quick,' Flo replied with disgust that she had absolutely no desire to bear witness to his **hypereccrisia**."

hyperemesis /hi per EM eh sis/ n • Abnormally profuse or prolonged vomiting.

"If only someone had warned Mary of the in-laws' cat's chronic **hyperemesis**, she would never have sported with it in such a rough-and-tumble fashion, and might have been spared the indignity of sitting through dinner with her husband's family while clad in a borrowed housedress several sizes too big."

(*compare **bespew, vomiturition***)

hyperemian /hype er EE mee an/ n • One who vomits excessively.

[Greek *hyper* above + *emesis* vomiting]

"Stuck for a name for their new multimillion-dollar backwards and upside-down roller coaster, amusement park officials considered dozens of choices before finally settling on 'The **Hyperemian**.'"

(*compare **bevomit, emetomaniac***)

hypergenitalism /hi per JEN it ull ism/ n • Overdevelopment of the genitals.

"Osgood's **hypergenitalism** did not pass unnoticed by

the talent scouts at the annual 'Please, Make Me a Star' convention in Pasadena."

(*compare **macrogenitosomia, macrophallus, mentulate***)

hypobulic /*hype o BOOL ik*/ adj • Unable to make decisions.
[Greek *hypo* under + *boule* will]

Paper or plastic? Chocolate or vanilla? Choice is a precious aspect of freedom, but to the **hypobulic** soul it can paradoxically be quite oppressive. If only they would repeat to themselves the following mantra: "It doesn't matter!"

hypogenitalism /*hi po JEN it ull ism*/ n • Stunted growth of the genitals.

"Little Chucky Stead had a hard life: the unrelenting acne, the layer of baby fat that just wouldn't go away, and worst of all, the severe **hypogenitalism** for which there was no remedy . . . would things ever get better?"

(*compare **microgenitalism***)

hypomaniac /*hype o MAY nee ak*/ n • A person with a mental disturbance characterized by excessive optimism.
[Greek *hypo* under + *mania* madness]

Supreme confidence, or **hypomania**? The line between the two is sometimes a fine one indeed. Take for example the prefight interview in which the unknown boxer about to be pulverized by the champion speaks hopefully about "fighting his fight" and so forth. Three minutes later, spitting out broken teeth, he says the ref stopped the match too soon. What is one to do with such people—admire them for their unconquerable spirit, or condemn them for their stupidity? Perhaps both.   (*compare **macromaniac***)

hypomazia /hi po MAY zee uh/ n • Underdevelopment of the breasts.

Lest the reader misinterpret the tone of this book, the authors offer the following clarification: We have nothing against small breasts. We have nothing against large breasts, or breasts of any kind.

(*compare* **macromastia, micromastia**)

· I ·

iatronudia /*eye at ro NOO dee uh*/ n • A woman's pretending to be ill out of a desire to disrobe in front of a doctor.

"There was something fishy here: after the young lady stripped naked to 'show him her hangnail,' Doctor Willoughby began to suspect he had a case of **iatronudia** on his hands." (*compare **apodyopsis***)

igly /*IG lee*/ adj • Extremely ugly.

Essentially, something qualifies as **igly** when it is uglier than ugly. (*compare **grizely***)

illitate /*ILL it ate*/ v • To overdecorate the female face.

Not to be confused with *irritate*, even though **illitating** might indeed irritate friends, husbands, or anybody with good taste.

imbonity /*im BON it ee*/ n • The absence of good qualities.
[Late Latin *imbonitas* evil condition]

Applicable to both persons and things, **imbonity** says it all. Consider the airplane meal that is late arriving, cold, tasteless, fattening, *and* too small. Or the Hollywood movie that is not only boring and offensive but over three hours long as well. These are all-too-common examples of modern-day **imbonity**. (*compare **shilpit***)

imbulbitate /*im BULB it ate*/ v • To defecate in one's pants.
[Latin *imbulbitare* to befoul, defile]
There really is no tiptoeing around the definition of this word.

" 'Oh, no!' " said Roscoe, as he tried in vain to extricate himself from between the elevator doors. 'Imbulbitated again!' " (*compare* **alacuoth, diamerdis**)

immerd /*im URD*/ v • To cover with excrement.
"No one claimed responsibility for **immerding** the supervisor's car, but suspicion immediately fell on Morgan, who was seen consuming copious quantities of coffee and pork rinds in the hours before the incident."

(*compare* **beray, bescumber, conskite, ordurous, sharny, shitten**)

imparlibidinous /*IM par lib ID in us*/ adj • Pertaining to an unequal state of desire between two people.
A word that gloriously and succinctly describes a state of affairs we all know far too well. When you ask the woman of your dreams out on a date and she laughs, spits on you, and says she would rather couple with a rhino, simply explain to your friends that the two of you were **imparlibidinous**.

impinguinate /*im PING win ate*/ v • To fatten.
"A jealous woman by nature, Yvette would cook an **impinguinating** dinner for her husband every night in the hope of making him less desirable to other women."

(*compare* **bariatrics, gavage**)

infandous /*IN fan duss*/ adj • Too odious to be spoken of.
[Latin *infandus* unspeakable]

Why is this word not more widely known? Perhaps because in this day and age there is simply *nothing* too odious to be splashed across a front page or made into a TV special, let alone spoken of. **Infandous** is a quaint old term hearkening back to a time when people actually knew shame.

The noun form of the word is **infandum.**

"J. Ackleby liked to sit back and ruminate over the many **infandous** stunts he'd pulled over the course of a long and fruitful career in publicity. It always brought a smile to his face to think of the time he'd entered the Siamese twins in the doubles open Ping-Pong tournament." (*compare vetanda*)

infausting /n FOSS ting/ adj • Inflicting bad luck upon others.

[Latin *infaustus* unfortunate]

"Craig loved taking his buddies out fishing in his boat, but whenever his pushy brother-in-law insisted on coming along no one caught any fish. One hot Sunday afternoon the men finally snapped, stranding the **infausting** fellow on a buoy with nothing but a bag of minnows and a transistor radio running low on batteries."

infibulate /in FIB yoo late/ v • To practice infibulation upon: to fit with a chastity belt or otherwise tie down, lock up, or sew shut a person's genitals to prevent him or her from having sex.

A word that might, for instance, be applied to that poor sap in college who, with his weasely face, flaccid physique, and chronic nasal drip, might as well have been **infibulated** for all the chance he had of getting laid.

"His political star had risen quickly among his conser-

infibulate

vative constituents, due in large measure to his calling for the **infibulation** of the state's many welfare recipients."

ingler /*ING ler*/ n • The passive participant in anal intercourse.

A versatile word, **ingler** can be either a mortal insult or a term of endearment, depending upon one's milieu.

(*compare **poger, sodomitess***)

initiatrix /*in ish ee AY trix*/ n • A female initiator.

A rather broad definition that lends itself to a specific and salacious inference.

"Charlie got a lot of money at his bar mitzvah, but the

best present didn't come in an envelope at all: his older brother took him to an **initiatrix** on the other side of town."

inkle /INK l/ v • To attend a party to which one has not been invited.

Sir Leslie so needed to tinkle
*that he soon attempted to **inkle***
a gala soiree
that turned him away,
so their hedgerows he did sprinkle.

(*compare **sorn***)

insiliarius /in SIL ee AIR ee us/ n • An evil advisor.

These saboteurs are usually hard to spot until after their damage is done, but can be useful once identified; just do the opposite of what they recommend.

"After he attempted to impress his beloved by lifting the dung cart—with disastrous results—Amos realized that as far as winning his heart's desire was concerned, his brother was an **insiliarius** whose advice was to be disregarded at all costs." (*compare **leguleian***)

intromission /in tro MISH un/ n • Insertion of the penis into the vagina.

At the theater, if they announced that there would be a short **intromission** between the acts, a good percentage of the audience might remain in their seats instead of ducking outside for a smoke.

"It was precisely at the moment of **intromission** that Bixby remembered he had neglected to turn off the coffee maker at work—things went downhill from there."

(*compare **irrumation***)

irrumate /ih roo MATE/ v • To insert one's penis into someone's mouth.

irrumation /ih roo MAY shun/ n • The act of **irrumating** (see above).

"He was a kind and sweet man, and their love affair would have lasted longer had he not been so brutishly persistent in his **irrumations**." (*compare **lecheur***)

· J ·

janiform /JAN *if orm*/ adj • Two-faced.

A word unsuitable for politicians, who after all have many more than just *two* faces.   (*compare* **fissilingual**)

jarble /JAR *bul*/ v • To spatter with something; wet; bemire.

"Roger cursed his unsteady hands; he had **jarbled** himself in the hotel bathroom, and now he was obliged to get up close and personal with the electric hand dryer."

(*compare* **lantrify**)

jehu /JAY *hoo*/ n • A reckless driver.

In ancient times, **Jehu** was a king of Israel known for his furious and daring chariot attacks. In modern parlance, this eponymous word denotes someone who should have his or her driver's license revoked.

"Veronica frequently found her eccentric stepfather to be a source of great embarrassment, and never more so than when he would drop her off at her high school. Often while she made her way through the parking lot to the front steps, he would lean out of his driver's side window, shaking his fist with rage at students who drove their own cars with what he decided was reckless abandon: "Damn you, you young jackanapes! You **jehus**!"

janiform

jobberknowle /*JOB er nowl*/ n • A heavy and dim-witted person.

It sounds rather like some fabulous creature out of nineteenth-century children's fiction, but alas, the **jobber-knowle** is about as ethereal as a tollbooth clerk. If the reader wishes to see one, all he or she has to do is call the phone company and ask to have another line installed; they'll send one right over. (*compare* **looby**)

jugulate /*JUG yoo late*/ v • To throttle or cut the throat of; attack by the neck; hang by the neck.

Finally, a word that covers any kind of neck attack. Talk about useful—however did we get by without **jugulate**?

jumentous /joo MENT us/ adj • Smelling like horse urine. Also, resembling horse urine in color and frothiness.

This delightful word is a wolf in sheep's clothing: it sounds festive and jolly, but actually has a stinking, disgusting meaning. That makes it perfect for undetectable insults: "This haggis is just **jumentous**," you might say, or "a **jumentous** time was had by all," or "I'd like to thank all of you for joining us on this most **jumentous** occasion."

· K ·

kakidrosis /*kak id RO sis*/ n • The secretion of foul-smelling perspiration.

"Although the ammonia carried with it a certain sting, Bruce found that nothing else could dampen his **kakidrosis**."
(*compare* **bromidrosis, podobromhidrosis**)

kakopygian /*kak o PIE gee an*/ adj • Possessing an ugly set of buttocks.

[Greek *kakos* bad + *pyge* rump]

This book contains words for nice asses, fat asses, and hairy asses, but consider for a moment the potential for overlap among these terms. After all, some people think that fat asses are nice, and there may even be some who are fond of hairy asses. In the interest of fairness, **kakopygian** is offered for anyone with a need to express his or her displeasure with someone's posterior.

"Jurgen Wallace had always been ahead of his time as a choreographer; some even called him a visionary. But the debut of his latest opus, 'The **Kakopygian's** Waddle,' ended in disaster when those members of the audience who did not flee in disgust charged the stage howling with fury, forcing his entire troupe to scurry to safety as best they could." (*compare* **apoglutic, unipygic**)

keck /KEK/ v • To attempt to vomit without success.

Even more onomatopoeic than the familiar, almost-synonomous *retch*.

"When the exact nature of the dumplings we had just eaten was made known to us there was a mad stampede for the bathroom, but alas, we could do no more than **keck**."

(compare ***vomiturition***)

kedge /KEJ/ v • To fill oneself with meat.

Kedge is not a particularly insulting word, but it certainly is unpleasant.

"Preston just could not pass up a bet involving food. As a result, he was now so thoroughly **kedged** that he could not leave the steak house under his own power, and was restricted to a vocabulary of grunts and moans."

(compare ***nidorosity***)

keech /KEECH/ n • A lump of rolled-up fat.

A small and ugly word. (compare ***fenks***)

klazomaniac /klaz o MAY nee ak/ n • A compulsive shouter; one who speaks entirely in shouts.

Whenever sharing space with a **klazomaniac** is unavoidable, it is best not to exercise any restraint in making your displeasure known. There is no reason why anyone, even if he is stone deaf, should yell directly and incessantly into your face. The idiot probably just loves the sound of his or her own voice. (compare ***cachinnator***)

kleptolagnia /klept o LAG nee uh/ n • Sexual excitement from stealing.

"Oswald's thievery grew to keep pace with his insatiable

kleptolagnia, until he began taking risks that culminated in his ignoble and acutely embarrassing apprehension."

*(compare **hybristophilia**)*

klismaphiliac /*kliz muh FEEL ee ak*/ n • A person with a sexual interest in receiving enemas.

King Louis XIV of France deserves special mention in any discussion of enemas. While it is not known if he obtained sexual gratification through the practice, he certainly took his irrigation seriously. He even had a special throne built so that he might continue with his cleansing while attending to matters of state. According to the written records of the time, he submitted to these internal ablutions more than two thousand times during his reign.

"Too ashamed to admit to anyone that he was a **klismaphiliac,** Mallory would go to absurd lengths to justify garnering himself an enema, often by consuming vast quantities of a homemade concoction of system-blocking foods mixed with sawdust."

*(compare **clyster, huskanoy**)*

knipperdollin /*nip er DOLL in*/ n • A fanatical idiot.

[From Bernhard Knipperdolling, fanatical leader of the Munster Anabaptists from 1533 to 1535]

This is a surprisingly useful word for what is potentially a very dangerous person. Although a case can be made that a fanatical idiot is less threatening than a clever one, are not all fanatics idiotic to some extent? This much is for sure: When confronted with a **knipperdollin,** there is no middle ground. One must either flee immediately, or send him off on a suicide mission posthaste.

*(compare **fanaticise, naffin**)*

kordax */KORE dax/* n • A penis dance performed by horned figures in the Dionysian festivals of ancient Greece.

"The PTA at our high school was dead set against having the students organize their own dance; to them, anything less sedate than foxtrot night might as well have been a **kordax**."

· L ·

lairwite /LAIR *white*/ n • A fine formerly levied for adultery.

"Not only did Trevor have to pay the **lairwite** as a result of his transgressions, but his wife dumped boiling water on his lap." (*compare* **lenocinium**)

lant /LANT/ n • Stale urine used in manufacturing.

That's right: manufacturing. What kind? Wool-scouring, for one. Happy?

"The labor dispute at the textile plant got really ugly after union workers began dunking their supervisors in the **lant** vat." (*compare* **lotium**)

lantrify /LANT *rif eye*/ v • To moisten with urine.

A unique and mystifying word. How many things are there that get moistened with urine routinely enough to have necessitated a term for this action? With luck, we shall never know.

"The cookbook had to be recalled when it was discovered that the recipe for chutney quiche on page 84 called for the **lantrifying** of the crust prior to baking. (It was, after all, supposed to be a *vegetarian* cookbook.)" (*compare* **bepiss**)

lapidable /LAP *id uh bul*/ adj • Worthy of being stoned.

If you are prevented by courtesy from expressing what

you really think of the meal, simply say "The chef is really quite **lapidable**."   (*compare **screable***)

lapidate /*LAP id ate*/ v • To stone; to kill by hurling rocks at.

"After Mike ran over the headman's favorite goat while stoned on hashish, it began to look like he would be **lapidated** by irate villagers."   (*compare **fustigate***)

lascivia /*luh SIV ee uh*/ n • Abnormally strong sexual desire.

Lascivia, then, is the condition of inordinate *lasciviousness*.

"Pomerantz's **lascivia** served him in good stead; when it was discovered, he was passed over for the eunuchs and placed instead in the queen's retinue."

(*compare **erotomania, satyriasis, tentigo***)

lask /*LASK*/ v • To be afflicted with diarrhea.

" 'I'm sorry,' said the secretary, 'but Mr. Cooper happens to be **lasking** at the moment. May I take a message?' "
(*compare **collywobbles***)

lecheur /*lay SHIRRH*/ n • A licker of genitals.

"Weights, yoga, intricate furniture arrangements— Peabody tried everything as part of his all-consuming ambition to be an auto-**lecheur**."   (*compare **irrumation***)

legruita /*LEG roo EET uh*/ n • A fine or penalty for undue familiarity with a woman.

"It became an infamous scam: Whenever the town's coffers ran low, the wily Marshal Blackstone would set out a string of well-baited **legruita** traps. It was never very long before much-needed revenue began pouring in."

(*compare **skimmington***)

leguleian /leg YOOL ee an/ n • A small-time lawyer. adj •
Resembling a lawyer.

[Latin *leguleius* a pettifogging lawyer]

This word more than fulfills the criteria of an insult, in
either its primary or secondary sense.

"With the sweat pouring off of him in the midday sun,
Milton's bewildered father vowed that he would never
again fall victim to one of his precocious son's **leguleian**
tricks for getting out of mowing the lawn."

(*compare **barrator, bdelloid, rabulistic***)

leint /LAINT/ v • To add urine to ale to make it stronger.

More than modern dentistry, or even the abolition of
debtors' prison, this appalling practice illustrates why it is
better to be alive today than in the eighteenth century: We
no longer feel the need to piss in our beer.

"'Would you like something stronger to go with that?'
the bartender asked the troubled salesman while drawing

leint

his ale from the tap. 'No,' came the reply. 'I'm off the rum tonight; just make sure you **leint** that pint before you serve it.'" (*compare **uriposiac***)

lenocinium /*len o SIN ee um*/ n • Accepting or encouraging infidelity in one's wife in return for monetary gain.

"The other men in the village might jeer him, but in the last year alone Walter had purchased a new cart, a slightly-

lenocinium

used plow, and several fine young hogs—and **lenocinium** had paid for it all." *(compare **wittol**)*

lickspigot /LIK *spig ot*/ n • A revolting parasite.
*The **lickspigot** lay anxious in wait*
for the diners to finish their date.
Their departure was sped
when he came up and said,
"Do you mind if I lick off your plate?"
*(compare **fart-sucker, scaff**)*

licktwat /LIK *twat*/ n • A term of contempt.

A word of genuine mystery, **licktwat** appears in numerous dictionaries but is never defined. Lexicographers seem content to list the word alone, trusting either to the inherent knowledge or the salacious imagination of their readers. Lacking an authoritative source, the authors are reluctant to assign it a specific meaning, and will list it only as a general term of opprobrium.

Of course, following the example set by numerous other words (**lickspigot,** *lickpenny,* etc.), one may safely assume that this word is not only a term of contempt, but a remarkably naughty one as well. Such words give the lie to the fallacious argument that the once-dignified English tongue is rapidly vulgarizing, for **licktwat** and many other terms just as salty are hundreds of years old. English is a filthy language, and always has been.

An interesting aside on the word *twat*: In a fairly infamous literary faux pas, Robert Browning once mistakenly used the word in a poem to refer to part of a nun's outfit. He made the error after reading this passage from *Vanity of Vanities* from 1660: "They talk't of his having a

Cardinall's hat, They'd send him as soon an Old Nun's Twat." *(compare **tittery-whoppet**)*

lientery /*LIE en teh reel*/ n • Diarrhea consisting of undigested or semidigested food.

"Howie's **lientery** might not have been quite so uncomfortable had he not consumed three jars of pigs' feet the night before." *(compare **chyme**)*

liffy /*LIFF ee*/ v • To seduce a woman with promises of fidelity, and then desert her.

"George wanted nothing so much as to be able to **liffy** every woman that he met. He was thwarted in his efforts, however, as even those few that he did succeed in bedding summarily dumped him immediately afterward."

Ed's fancy being smitten
by a saucy pert young kitten,
he wooed her on the phone
and dodged her chaperone.
After deflowering his dame,
Ed soon tired of the game.
His conscience being iffy,
*he decided he would **liffy***
and try his luck again. *(compare **legruita**)*

limberham /*LIM ber ham*/ n • An obsequious, servile person.

Who needs yoga? The **limberham** is supple-jointed from bowing and scraping.

"Sanford's waiter turned out to be such a simpering **limberham** that it made him feel profoundly uncomfortable. Halfway through his dinner he saw no alternative but to begin abusing him terribly—anything to stop that horrible fawning." *(compare **fart-sucker, timeserver**)*

liffy

limitarian /*lim it AIR ee an*/ n • One who believes that salvation is restricted to a certain group of individuals.

These self-righteous religious exclusionists have caused a lot of trouble over the centuries. Maybe there ought to be a special section reserved for them in Hell.

(*compare **antinomian***)

lipophilic /*lip o FILL ik*/ adj • Having an affinity for fat. [Greek *lipos* fat + *philein* to love]

Although this is a medical term, **lipophilic** may have uses above and beyond those it has heretofore known. Specifically, it could be applied to those people who demonstrate a proclivity for members of the opposite sex who can only be described as obese.

"Most of his fellow construction workers also favored women of above-average heft, but the **lipophilic** Luiz would grunt excitedly at only the most corpulent specimens of femininity, and, staring at their posteriors as they walked by, exclaim, 'Unh! Baby! It looks like two ten-years-olds fightin' under a blanket!'" *(compare **engrease**)*

lobcock /LOB *cock*/ n • A stupid, clumsy person.

"'You stupid, clumsy man,' cried the vicar's wife after Maynard broke his third piece of china, 'why, you're nothing but a **lobcock**!'" *(compare **asshead**)*

looby /LOO *bee*/ n • An awkward, unwieldy oaf; often stupid and lazy as well.

"'Well I'll be,' drawled Willie's gym teacher, pointing up at the terrified teen. 'That **looby** on the knotted rope is funnier-lookin' than a monkey tryin' to fuck a greased football! Let's keep 'im up there!'" *(compare **jobberknowle**)*

lotium /LO *shum*/ n • Stale urine formerly used by barbers as a cosmetic for the hair.

Lotium is Latin for urine.

"Imagine Allison's profound unease when she discovered her roommate had been spiking the house shampoo with her own homemade **lotium**." *(compare **lant**)*

lovertine /LUV *er teen*/ adj • Addicted to sex.

Describing someone as **lovertine** sounds so much more

lotium

poetic than calling them a raving sex maniac, doesn't it?

(*compare* **philopornist**)

lubbard /*LUB ard*/ n • An idle fellow; a man who could work, but doesn't.

[Middle English *lobre* a fat lazy fellow]

"Being profiled in ***Lubbard's Life*** magazine filled Maxwell with a sense of pride: the same kind he got from a job well shirked. There he was on the cover, big as life, grinning as he posed outside his home—grandpa's toolshed—under the caption 'It takes a real man not to work.'"

(*compare **egrote***)

lubbard

· M ·

mab /*MAB*/ v • To dress oneself in a careless manner.

"For the third time in a week, Lindsey slept right through his alarm clock. Now he had just enough time to splash his face, **mab,** and dash off to catch the crowded train to work. Squeezing into the car just as the doors closed, he beheld a sea of silent staring faces, which alerted him to the fact that he had no pants on."

(*compare* **bedizen**)

macrogaster /*MAK ro gas ter*/ n • A person with a big belly.

One of the ironies of today is that so many of those who freely dispense pompous bits of advice on how to eat healthily are **macrogasters** themselves.

"Drawing inspiration from such eclectic sources as hospital maternity gowns and butcher's smocks, Flavian made a killing with a line of clothes specifically designed for the hip young **macrogasters** of today." (*compare* **draffsack**)

macrogenitosomia /*MAK ro jen it o SO mee uh*/ n • Oversized penis in a newborn.

Blessing or curse? You decide.

"To their collective revulsion, the nurses in the maternity ward realized that the extra swagger in the step of the

mab

macrogaster

vile and loathsome Mr. Perkins was actually a reaction to his newborn son's **macrogenitosomia**."

macromaniac /MAK ro MAY nee ak/ n • One under the delusion that a part of his or her body is larger than it actually is.

[Greek *makros* long + *mania* madness]

"An incurable **macromaniac**, J.C. was never bothered by the peals of feminine laughter that accompanied his every striptease. And with all the sympathy tips he collected from patrons who took pity on him, he wound up earning more than any other male exotic dancer in the club."

(*compare* **brachyphallic**)

macromastia /MAK ro MAST ee uh/ n • The development of abnormally large breasts.

"It was as the surgeon explained to her that the implants came in three sizes—Large, Extra Large, and **Macromastia**—that Jill first began to have her doubts about the operation." (*compare **bathycolpian, mammose***)

macrophallus /*mak ro FAL us*/ n • An inordinately large penis.

"While he knew his was no **macrophallus,** Montgomery had always hoped that in the dark no one would be the wiser." (*compare **byental, mentulate, microphallus***)

mageira /*muh JY ruh*/ n • A woman's sublimation of sexual desire through cooking.

"Sex was okay, but what Marty really liked was eating, and to this end he fostered his wife's **mageira** by making love to her as infrequently as possible."

malversation /*mal ver ZAY shun*/ n • Corruption in office; misuse of public funds.

"The citizens at the town meeting bristled with indignation when it was revealed that the bulk of the newly uncovered **malversation** had gone toward providing psychological counseling for the mayor's three spoiled children, in the wake of the episode when they set the mailman's truck on fire." (*compare **empleomaniac***)

mammose /*mam OSE*/ adj • Having an ample bosom.

A perfectly serviceable little word for massive melons.

" 'Were Madame not quite so . . . **mammose,**' said Victor the tailor tactfully, 'a size three would certainly have been *plausible . . .*' " (*compare **bathycolpian, macromastia***)

mammothrept /*MAM o thrept*/ n • A spoiled child.

From the Greek *mammothreptos* (a child raised by its grandmother).

"Dr. Luetic's revolutionary book on child rearing, *Subdue Your Kid!* became a runaway best-seller when word got out that he recommended the severe paddling of **mammothrepts.**" (*compare* **misopedia**)

mangonist /*MAN gon ist*/ n • One who dresses up inferior wares for sale.

mangonist

"Spit and elbow grease were fine for all those mom-and-pop-type antique stores that sold heirloom silver, but Emilio the **mangonist** found that painting his wares with a pewterlike gloss and issuing seals of authenticity worked just as well."   (*compare* **comprachico, grimthorpe**)

maritality /*ma rih TAL it ee*/ n • Excessive fondness for one's husband.

"With the knowledge that she gleaned from her week at the self-awareness seminar, Joy returned home with a steely resolve not to give her undeserving husband the **maritality** he had come to expect. Instead, she would dote on her shih tzu."   (*compare* **mariturient**)

maritodespotism /*mar it o DESS pot ism*/ n • Ruthless domination of a wife by her husband.

"Ned's attempts to usher in a new era of **maritodespotism** to his marriage backfired badly, as his wife—who had previously ignored him—now began to beat him regularly."   (*compare* **cagamosis**)

mariturient /*ma rih TYOO ree ent*/ adj • Desiring to become a husband.

There is nothing wrong with being just a bit **mariturient.** But any quality, no matter how sterling it might be, can be taken to unreasonable lengths.

"**Mariturient** at any cost, Lincoln displayed a desperation that paid dividends of misery in the long run. His shrewish bride knew from the start that she was doing him a tremendous favor by marrying him, and she never let him forget it."   (*compare* **maritality**)

marplot /MAR plot/ n • A person who interferes; one who ruins the best-laid plans.

"The wrestling team at Northanger High wasn't pleased to have their closed-door locker-room romps exposed to the rest of the school, and thus few were surprised when they grabbed the **marplot** from the student newspaper, wrapped him head to toe in adhesive tape, and stuck him in a rather small locker, forgetting that a long weekend was coming up."

martext /MAR text/ n • A blundering preacher.

"The **martext** presiding at the wedding arrived late and drunk, lost his place several times during his rambling speech, and needed to be propped up by a groomsman. Just when it seemed like things couldn't get any worse, he called the bride by the wrong name during the exchange of vows, and it began to look like Julian would never get to marry his high school sweetheart after all."

maschalephidrosis /mass kuh lef id RO sis/ n • Runaway armpit perspiration.

"Although the woman at the pharmacy looked at him oddly when he bought multiple boxes of superabsorbent panty liners, Hugo had found that nothing less could handle the task of mopping up his **maschalephidrosis**."
   (compare **bromidrosis, hircismus, podobromhidrosis**)

mastigophoric /mass tig o FOR ik/ adj • Whip-wielding.

"The Duchovnys were a rather eccentric couple, as could be inferred from the blown-up photo of a leering Mrs. Duchovny, *in delicato* and **mastigophoric**, dominating the dining room."   (compare **algolagnia**)

mastoptosis /*mass TOE TOE sis*/ n • Sagging, pendulous breasts.

"Liza's boyfriend liked her **mastoptosis;** she, on the other hand, found letting out all her bras to be an enormous hassle." (*compare* **mazopexy**)

mattoid /*MAT oid*/ n • A semi-insane person.

[Latin *mattus* stupid, drunk]

A word for a semi-insane person is long overdue. **Mattoid** comes to us via the medical profession, where it refers to a specific diagnosis. Might it not be better used to describe those people who have something odd about them that one can't quite put one's finger on (until a switch gets thrown and they go bananas)?

"The fur muffler worn in July should have been a tip-off, but Brenda was feeling frisky, so she struck up a conversation with the **mattoid** sitting next to her on the train. It soon became evident that this had been a serious error in judgment." (*compare* **crackheaded, naffin**)

matutolagnia /*may too toe LAG nee uh*/ n • The desire to have sex in the morning.

"After his wife's **matutolagnia** made him miss his fourth consecutive morning meeting, George started looking for work as a night watchman." (*compare* **dysania**)

mazopexy /*MAZE o pex ee*/ n • Surgery to lift sagging breasts.

"His business was listed under 'Body Enhancements,' but the Hollywood cognoscenti knew him as the **mazopexist** to the stars." (*compare* **mastoptosis**)

mazophilous /*maze o FIL us*/ adj • Fond of breasts.

"His friends all thought that Humphrey was too overtly **mazophilous,** and they were secretly amused when he had all of his fingers viciously broken after he proved it with the wrong woman."   (*compare **pygophilous***)

meable /*MEE uh bull*/ adj • Easily penetrated.

Meable does not have an overtly sexual definition, but lends itself so perfectly to innuendo that the distinction is moot. Use this word as you see fit; we hope you'll have many an opportunity to do so.   (*compare **peccable***)

meconium /*meh KONE ee um*/ n • A baby's first feces after being born; a dark green tarlike excretion containing mucus, bile, and shed cells.

None of the medical literature consulted addresses the central question: Does it stink, or does that come later?
                                                      (*compare **steatorrhea***)

megarectum /*MEG uh REK tum*/ n • A rectum that is overly dilated.

"Proud possessor of a **megarectum,** Alphonse put it to lucrative use in such underground cinema classics as *Chambre à Louer* (Room to Spare) and *Chatouille-Moi à L'Intérieur* (Tickle Me Inside)."

meldrop /*MEL drop*/ n • A drop of liquid suspended at the end of the nose.

"He was one of those sad and undersized schoolboys, always with a **meldrop** that he would periodically wipe on his sleeve."   (*compare **snurt***)

mentulate /MENT yoo late/ adj • Possessing a large penis.

"Being **mentulate** wasn't always everything it was cracked up to be, mused Barney; indeed, it was often the height of inconvenience."

*(compare **macrophallus**)*

merdivore /MURD iv or/ n • An eater of excrement.

In English we have many words that relate to the eating of shit, and guess what? We need every damn one of them.

"We were all a bit put off when our host—after an admittedly delicious stew—began extolling the virtues of a **merdivorous** diet: 'Why look at those fellows, the dung beetles,' he said, 'strong as oxen, they are!'"

*(compare **coprophagist, scatophage**)*

merdurinous /murd YOO rin us/ adj • Made up of urine and feces.

The reader may well decide to use this word in a metaphorical sense, perhaps to describe vile-tasting food of an indeterminate consistency. *(compare **urinous**)*

meretriculate /meh ruh TRIK yoo late/ v • To deceive, as does a whore.

How exactly does a whore deceive? It might be in any one of a number of ways. She (or he) could pretend to be of a different sex, for example, or welsh on a payment made in advance. Presumably, a whore might even represent herself or himself as having greater sexual prowess than is in fact the case. In any event, since the authors unfortunately do not have information at their disposal to further elucidate this verb and are sorely lacking in personal experience in this area, readers are advised to use

meretriculate as best they see fit, to describe the actions of various species, male or female, that they disapprove of.

(*compare* **chrematisophiliac**)

merkin /MUR *kin*/ n • A pussy wig; artificial hair for the female pudendum.

While it may seem that we have no real need for such an article today, at one time **merkins** were greatly in demand. On the French Can-Can stage, for example, dancers who could flash a wisp or two of pubic hair had, shall we say, a leg up on the competition. Since some women lacked the requisite hair, there arose a market for **merkins**.

"Françoise was overjoyed; after many long months of scrimping and saving, she could finally afford that luxurious

merkin

new **merkin** she'd had her eye on, and throw away the cheap, itchy one that she'd bought in the thrift store on the Rue St. Denis." *(compare **tittery-whoppet**)*

metapneustic /*met uh NEW stik*/ adj • Breathing through an apparatus located in the anus, as with some insects.

Metapneustic is a word that, while it is intended to describe insects, with a small stretch can also be applied to people, in particular those individuals with their heads stuck firmly up their asses.

meteorism /*MEE tee or ism*/ n • Bloating in the abdomen due to gas.

"After the extra buoyancy granted him by his **meteorism** saved his life in the whitewater rafting accident, Cosgrove resolved to eat as much cheese as he liked."
*(compare **bdolotic, carminative, flatus**)*

meupareunia /*moo per ROO nee uh*/ n • Sexual activity in which only one partner is gratified.

"A legal precedent was set that day, as the jury agreed that Mrs. Grimthorpe's savage mutilation of her husband while he slept was indeed justified, due to her years of **meupareunia** at his hands." *(compare **artamesia**)*

micrencephalus /*mike ren SEF uh lus*/ n • A person with an abnormally small brain.

An authoritative-sounding word to describe stupid people, such as clerks at the DMV, and insurance salesmen of any kind. *(compare **excerebrose**)*

microgenitalism /*mike ro JEN it ul ism*/ n • A condition in which the genitals are inordinately small.

"Roland, already known to suffer from **microgenitalism** of the first order, suffered another grievous setback to his sex life with the accident on the diving board, in which he bit off the front third of his tongue."

(*compare* ***hypogenitalism***)

micromania /*mike ro MAY nee uh*/ n • The delusion that a part of one's body has shrunk or is in danger of shrinking.

This is the closest word we have in English to the uniquely Chinese *koro,* the widespread hysterical conviction that one's penis is shrinking. *Koro* is recorded to have swept entire regions, driving men into such a panic that they would don protective bamboo devices before going to bed in order to guard against the disappearance of their members overnight.　　　　　　　(*compare* ***tarassis***)

micromaniac /*mike ro MAY nee ak*/ n • A victim of micromania; a person under the delusion that a part of his body has shrunk.

"After viewing the evidence, the judges agreed that Hannibal the **micromaniac** had definitely been the victim of a spell of belittlement. The decision was made to burn the witches."

micromastia /*mike ro MASS tee uh*/ n • The condition of having tiny breasts.

"Some thought it inappropriate for him to advertise his breast implant practice just outside the Center for **Micromastia,** but Dr. Anderson Lee didn't care: he was rich and getting richer."　　　(*compare* ***amastia, hypomazia***)

micropenis /*MIKE ro PEE niss*/ n • A penis that is less than two centimeters long.

There are many words in the English language for small penises—and those endowed with them. **Micropenis** stands out (or doesn't stand out) because of its remarkably specific definition. We've all heard various well-intentioned sex experts declare that the size of the penis is not the most important thing, but we have yet to hear any of them say that they would like to trade places with a man who has a **micropenis.** (*compare* **brachyphallic, peniculas, subvirate**)

microphallus /*mike ro FAL us*/ n • An abnormally small penis.

"In a pitiable effort to rectify his **microphallus,** Lewis bought a suction pump at a garage sale. The results were not encouraging." (*compare* **macrophallus, microgenitalism**)

micturient /*mik TYOO ree ent*/ adj • Feeling a strong desire to urinate.

The next time you are in polite company and feel the call of nature, instead of saying you have to tinkle, take a leak, or drain your hog, why not take the classy route and say you feel **micturient**?

"Being unbearably **micturient** just at the climax of the movie, Cooper thought it perfectly acceptable to relieve himself into his empty popcorn bucket; his date was less than understanding."

micturition /*mik choo RISH un*/ n • Excessively frequent urination.

The Latin *mingo* (to urinate) is the root of both **micturition** and **micturient.**   (*compare* **polakuiria**)

milt /*MILT*/ n • Fish semen.

Caviar is a highly esteemed delicacy—why is it that no one eats **milt**? Perhaps because the very notion is revolting.

"Pierre was a true gastronomic adventurer, but even he recoiled from the offering of **milt** on a biscuit."

misandrist /*MIZ and rist*/ n • A hater of men.

This is the counterpart to the well-known *misogynist* (hater of women). A **misandrist** is characterized by **misandry.**

"Lily made a sizable fortune running a dating school that taught wealthy and conversationally inept men how to behave in order to snare a partner. Unfortunately, the experience caused her to become a lifelong **misandrist,** and she wound up retiring to live in the woods with her three cats." (*compare **novercant***)

misologist /*miz ALL uh jist*/ n • One with a hatred of mental activity.

In these days of television, computer games, and widespread "dumbing down," the **misologists** are in the majority.

"The store manager gave Dotti an abacus when the cash register broke down, but as a lifelong **misologist** she just couldn't be bothered trying to learn to use it."

(*compare **excerebrose, witling***)

misopedia /*miz o PEE dee uh*/ n • An intense, unreasonable hatred of children, especially one's own.

Misopedia does not refer to the regular, run-of-the-mill dislike we all have for the little monsters—which is, of course, normal—but only to an unusually intense and unreasonable hatred.

"As part of his revolutionary new aversion therapy for **misopedia,** Dr. Schneider would handcuff his patients to the backstop during Sunday Little League games."

(*compare **mammothrept***)

misopedia

mome /MOME/ n • A nitpicking critic.

[Anglicized form of *Momus,* the Greek god of ridicule]

A new four-letter word is a pretty rare find; one with a stinging definition, rarer still. What a treat, then, to encounter **mome** for the first time.

"Having milked his crude dung sculptures for all the free publicity a drummed-up controversy could muster, Antoine, the hip and thoroughly untalented new artist, needed a new gimmick. But when people reacted with boredom to his vomit paintings, he lashed out cattily, saying, 'Everybody's a **mome.**'" (*compare* **zoilus**)

monorchid /*mon OR kid*/ n • A man with one testicle. adj • Having only one testicle.

"After the badminton accident left him a **monorchid,** Mr. Spratwell flatly told his wife that their days of making love every morning and evening were over: 'I've got to conserve my fluids, dear,' he said, 'and I'm working at half-speed.'" (*compare* **triorchid**)

monotonist /*mon* OT *un ist*/ n • A person who constantly speaks on only one subject.

It takes time to realize that the person one is talking to is a **monotonist.** Suspicion may arise after just a few minutes, but one does not know for sure until several hours have passed. By then it is too late; one has already squandered a small but precious portion of one's life on an intolerable bore.

"As his stultifying date with Sophie dragged into its third hour, Sam realized why this stunning woman did not have a boyfriend: She was a horrible **monotonist** whose conversation consisted entirely of endless prattle about her collection of pewter figurines."

mouchard /*moo* SHARD/ n • A spy in the employ of the police.

While **mouchard** will probably never replace "rat" in gangster lingo, one cannot deny that the word does have a certain panache.

"Throughout the East End, the name 'Steven Abramowitz' struck fear into the hearts of all the other criminals and riffraff. He was rumored to have once drowned a man in a urinal. What was not known, however, was that he was also a **mouchard** who would drop a dime on his own grandmother if it would keep the bobbies from shutting down his underground bingo empire."

mulierose /MOO lee er ose/ adj • Addicted to the love of women.

"Ivan had been **mulierose** for so long, he thought of it as a way of life. Then he met Cleo, the transvestite with a voice of silver and a heart of gold, and he enjoyed their fleeting romance so much that it prompted a midlife crisis he never fully worked through."   (compare **raddled**)

mumblecrust /MUM bl crust/ n • A toothless old beggar.

Some readers might think it rather cruel to refer to a toothless old beggar as a **mumblecrust**. The authors disagree. Attention, all you bleeding hearts out there! (In the unlikely event that any of you are still with us this far into the book.) We say that the word **mumblecrust** can be employed with sensitivity and understanding.

"Get out of my store, you foul **mumblecrust**!" shrieked the fishmonger's wife. She had caught the tattered hobo eyeing a pocket-sized perch, and was now chasing after him with a broom, raising clouds of dust and fleas in the process."   (compare **cadator**)

mumchance /MUM chance/ n • A silent numbskull. v • To remain silent due to caution or stupidity.

"The professor had a sadistic side, and would always ferret out the **mumchances** in his class early enough to afford himself a full semester devoted to teasing and humiliating them."   (compare **witling**)

muscod /MUSS cod/ n • A perfumed fop; a man who wears too much scent.

Much as spices were originally sought out to mask the taste of spoiled meat, so was perfume developed to hide the stench of people's unwashed bodies. As we in civilized society have grown more conversant with the notion of personal hygiene, one would imagine that the need for perfume would diminish. But while some people have accepted this, there are plenty of others who seem to feel it is their primary duty in life to sail about assaulting the olfactory senses of their fellows.

"Vincent loved the smell of his aftershave, but was always somewhat disappointed when its sharp, tangy scent would begin to fade away twenty minutes or so after he put it on. Reasoning that if he couldn't smell it, it wasn't working, the **muscod** typically slathered on a quarter of a bottle at a time." (*compare **odorivector, stinkard***)

myatonia /*my uh TONE ee uh*/ n • Flabbiness; lack of muscular fitness.

"Such was Gustave's **myatonia** that a schoolmate of his once remarked that his entire body seemed to be constructed out of ass cheeks." (*compare **pyriform***)

myrmidon /*MUR mid on*/ n • A ruthless follower.

A word of classical origin: In Homer's *Iliad*, the **Myrmidons** were the brutal and fanatically obedient warrior followers of Achilles. According to myth, Zeus created them out of ants as subjects for Achilles' grandfather, King Aeacus. Aeacus beheld an anthill, and every ant became a **Myrmidon**. (*compare **fanaticise, knipperdollin***)

mysophiliac /*miz o FEEL ee ak*/ n • A person who is sexually excited by filth or excretions.

"Ruth wished that she had listened to the admonitions of her hippie parents, who warned her that while it was fine to experiment, she would eventually grow out of her **mysophiliac** phase. Living in a yurt behind the abattoir with the town garbage-picker was beginning to lose some of its charm." (*compare **eproctolagniac***)

· N ·

naffin /NAFF in/ n • One who is almost an idiot.

Some recipes call for garlic; for others, shallots will do. When the word *idiot* is a little too strong for the occasion, try **naffin** instead.

"Ever since the sad day poor old Fenton fell off the church steeple, the town fathers had been seeking a replacement for their beloved village idiot. Qualified applicants were hard to find, however, and the townsfolk had to suffer through a series of make-do **naffins** in the meantime." (*compare **dunderwhelp, mattoid***)

nanophilia /nan o FEEL ee uh/ n • A lust for short people.

"Pasqual was crushed when his wife informed him that she could no longer combat the **nanophilia** raging in her veins, and was running off to join the much-celebrated dwarf circus."

natiform /NAT if orm/ adj • Shaped like the buttocks.

Off the top of one's head, it is difficult to think of something that cries out to be described as **natiform**. No matter; this word is obviously not complimentary, and opportunities to employ it will surely arise.

"The team of explorers felt a collective shiver run down their spines. Stretched before them was a sight never before

naffin

nanophilia

seen by Western eyes: the mating grounds of the fabled and **natiform** Butter Pygmies."

(*compare **apoglutic, kakopygian, unipygic***)

neanilagnia /*nee AN il AG nee uh*/ n • A sexual longing for young women.

"It was obvious to the kids in her sixth period gym class that Mrs. McGillucuddy suffered from more than a touch of **neanilagnia**." (*compare **anililagnia, gerontophilia***)

necrosadism /*nek ro SADE ism*/ n • Sexual gratification from the mutilation of dead bodies.

Many people think *necrophilia* (having sex with dead

people) is about as depraved as a word can possibly get—not so! **Necrosadism** ups the ante.

*(compare **algolagnia**)*

neoteny /*nee OT en ee*/ n • The retention of juvenile characteristics into adulthood.

"When he awoke the morning after his fortieth birthday with a truly meaningful hangover, strapped to the remains of what had once been his waterbed, Wedgewood thought to himself, 'This **neoteny** must end.'"

*(compare **anaclitic**)*

nidorosity /*nide or OSS it ee*/ n • A belch that tastes of cooked meat.

"Beads of perspiration began appearing on Terri's forehead, not because the waltz was tiring, but because she had to hold her breath to avoid inhaling her partner's **nidorosities**." *(compare **eructation, fumosities**)*

nihilarian /*NAI ih LAIR ee an*/ n • A person with a meaningless job.

"Having trouble dragging yourself to the office? Depressed because your job is a pointless treadmill? Don't be glum! **Nihilarian** Career Services can help. We train thousands for exciting careers in such fields as iguana grooming, figurine arranging, and electric toothbrush repair. Send for our free brochure today!"

*(compare **aidle, fustilarian, ploiter**)*

nimgimmer /*NIM gim er*/ n • A physician who specializes in the treatment of venereal disease.

"After losing his license to practice medicine because of

abuse of anesthesia, Lester was forced to become a back-alley **nimgimmer**." (*compare* *fireship*)

nisus /NIZE *us*/ n • The physical exertion involved in defecation, including the contraction of the abdominal muscles and the diaphragm. Also, the urge to mate in the spring, or any strong urge.

"It didn't matter how much oat bran and prune juice Jonathan consumed; even the most vein-popping **nisus** couldn't expel the blockage from his system."

(*compare* **tenesmus, vernalagnia**)

nocturia /nok TYOO *ree uh*/ n • Copious nocturnal urination.

"The omnipresent roar of nearby Niagara Falls may have had something to do with it, but whatever the reason, on his honeymoon Harry's **nocturia** reached a new level of inconvenience." (*compare* **enuresis**)

novercant /NO *ver kant*/ adj • Behaving like a stepmother.

"It was only her third date with their father, and already Ingrid was addressing the twins in severe, **novercant** tones, admonishing them not to wipe their mouths on their sleeves and the like. When the clumsy busboy spilled the hot tea on her lap, they could not contain their glee."

(*compare* **misandrist**)

nullimitus /null IM *it us*/ n • A male virgin.

"Sick and tired of being the only **nullimitus** in his social circle, one evening Samuel got drunk enough to drive down to Tijuana to rectify the situation. Before he knew what was happening, he was on stage in a strip club, bound and gagged, while a mustachioed grandmother had her way with him."   (*compare* **demivierge, subvirate**)

nympholepsy /NIM *fo lep see*/ n • An erotic daydream trance.

A person under the spell of **nympholepsy** is known as a *nympholept.*

"Lionel was rudely awakened from his **nympholepsy** by the teacher calling him up to the blackboard to solve a lengthy algebra problem, and had to scramble to cover his excitement with a textbook."

obsolagnium /*ob so LAG nee um*/ n • The fading of sexual desire in old age.

"Much to the shock and dismay of the young golddigger who had married him, the ancient and humpbacked Mr. Finch showed absolutely no sign whatsoever of any **obsolagnium**." (*compare **phallorhiknosis***)

obstipation /*ob stip AY shun*/ n • Stubborn and persistent constipation.

Just think "obstinate constipation."

"Ester was grateful for the **obstipation** she came down with on the camping trip, for she was not too keen on using leaves." (*compare **dejector***)

odorivector /*O dor ih VEK tor*/ n • The source of a smell.

Ah, the source of a smell. The fragrant rose; the pine woods in springtime; the loaf of fresh-baked bread. But let us leave these pleasant aromas behind for a moment, and turn instead to those offensive odors whose source is our fellow man.

Smell is invisible, and everyone is born immune to his own fetid emanations. That is why we often find ourselves looking an unwitting **odorivector** in the eye while straining not to breathe or audibly choke. It is a difficult posture to maintain, as the urge to flee or to douse the guilty party with a bucketful of mouthwash quickly builds.

"Although they tried to make the best of things, summertime just wasn't the same at the inner-city day camp after the budget cuts took hold. Instead of taking the kids swimming, counselors would march them to the public library to play 'find the **odorivector.**' "

*(compare **autosmia, diamerdis, muscod**)*

oikiomiasmata */oy kee o mee AZ mut uh/* n • Unhealthy domestic gases; wafting pollution in a household.

The odd-looking word **oikiomiasmata** also possesses an eccentric definition: bad smells resulting from shoddy housekeeping. It comes from the combination of the Greek *oikos* (house) and *miasmata* (pollution). And it is more useful than one may think at first glance.

"Christine couldn't live with the unbearable **oikiomiasmata** any longer: although it meant losing the silent battle of wills with her brother, she decided to take out the garbage." *(compare **effluvium**)*

omnifutuant */om nee FOO tyoo ant/* adj • Prone to engage in sexual activity with anything.

"Many readers were puzzled by the ad that ran in the Personals for several weeks that spring: 'Single Male **Omnifutuant,** seeking entity for romance on hot summer nights. Sex, age, species unimportant. Breathes oxygen a plus.' "

*(compare **animalist, anthropozoophilic, avisodomy, hippomanic**)*

oniomaniac */o nee o MAY nee ak/* n • A person with an unreasonable and uncontrollable impulse to buy things.

"Spending money was the only thing that Rupert's **onio-maniac** wife enjoyed doing, and even though the bills she ran up threatened to ruin him, he just didn't have the heart to take away her shopping privileges. He finally settled on buying the woman her own department store."

(*compare* **pleonexia**)

ophelimity /o *fuh* LIM *it ee*/ n • The ability to please one's sexual partner.

As it happens, **Ophelimity** can be wholly or partially impeded by various phenomena discussed in this book, such as **colpoxerosis** and **microphallus**.

"Where the questionnaire asked her to rate her husband's **ophelimity** on a scale of one to ten, Belinda checked 'Does Not Apply.'" (*compare* **anaphrodisiac**)

opisthotonicke /o PISS *tho* TON *ik*/ n • A short-necked person.

"What a coup for Julie and her sorority sisters! Finally one of their mixers had attracted the biggest prize of all: a pod of beer-guzzling, butt-pinching **opisthotonickes** from the varsity football team. Her heart swelled with pride."

(*compare* **brachyphallic**)

ordured /or DURED/ adj • Covered, spattered, or filled with dung. (*compare* **beray, bescumber, conskite, immerd, sharny, shitten**)

ordurous /or DURE *us*/ adj • Resembling dung; filthy.

"The kitchen staff was somewhat miffed when Mrs. Pendleton sent back the squab—haughtily referring to it as 'simply **ordurous**'—and each one of them eagerly contributed a gob of spit to her next course."

(*compare **fecaloid, stercoraceous***)

orf /ORF/ n • A sheep-borne skin disease that causes red, oozing sores around the mouth. No treatment is necessary; the condition eventually clears up by itself.

"Jamie wasn't about to let a little thing like a case of **orf** keep him from attending the shepherd's ball."

osphresiophilia /*oss free zee o FIL ee uh*/ n • Sexual excitement from smells.

"Being a perfume tester was a dream job for a woman with **osphresiophilia,** but Nancy's frequent trips to the bathroom began to raise some eyebrows in the lab."

(*compare **renifleur***)

ozoamblyrosis /*o zo am blih RO sis*/ n • The loss of sexual desire due to the unpleasant body odor of one's partner.

"Beatrice wished that being a marriage counselor was always this easy. Immediately upon meeting Mr. Simpson she knew the problem had to be **ozoamblyrosis,** so she handed Mrs. Simpson a pair of nose plugs and spent the rest of the hour getting a pedicure."

(*compare **osphresiophilia***)

· P ·

pageism /*PAGE ism*/ n • A mental disorder in which a man yearns to be the slave of a beautiful woman.

"Randal was a pasty man with a severe case of **pageism,** and while finding a woman willing to dominate him was easy, finding one who was also beautiful was proving to be a bit of a problem."   (*compare* **retifism**)

pandy /*PAN dee*/ v • To punish someone by beating them on the hands with a stick.

"Mrs. Hedley was generally regarded as a strict disciplinarian who got results, but when she avowed the return of **pandying** for her kindergarten class the school board began to weigh her dismissal."

(*compare* **bastinado, ferule**)

paphian /*PAY fee en*/ adj • Having to do with illicit love; pertaining to harlots; licentious; lewd.

"Gathered 'round the bonfire at night, the young campers loved to listen to farmer John's tales of wily foxes and savage bears. But when he burst into tears one evening and recounted the story of his **paphian** romance with Elsa, the winsome young sheep, the children all felt a bit odd."

paracoita /*para KOY tuh*/ n • A female sex partner.

"Webster couldn't lie to his mother, so he told her the box at the foot of his bed contained an inflatable **paracoita,** and left it at that."

paraphiliac /*para FIL ee ak*/ n • A person addicted to unorthodox sexual practices.

"At his first meeting of **Paraphiliacs** Anonymous, Wexler learned that he wasn't the only person in the world to have fallen head over heels for a small Ming vase."

(*compare **varietist***)

parbreak /*PAR brake*/ v • To vomit. n • Vomit.

Parbreaking on the golf course, unfortunately, will do little to lower one's score.

(*compare **copremesis, hyperemesis***)

parepithymia /*pa rep ith EYE mee uh*/ n • Perverted cravings due to mental illness.

"Faced with the prospect of losing his girlfriend's **parepithymia** due to her psychiatrist's meddling, Gavin took action and replaced her prescription medication with harmless little sugar pills."

(*compare **hogminny***)

parnel /*par NEL*/ n • The mistress of a priest.

For those men of the cloth for whom a **gugusse** is just not good enough, there is always a **parnel.** Derived via the French from the Latin *Petronilla* (Peter's woman).

"Father Nelson kept promising to leave the faith for his long-suffering **parnel,** but never mustered enough courage to make the move."

(*compare **gugusse***)

pathodixiac /*path o DIX ee ak*/ n • One who pretends to be ill in order to garner sympathy.

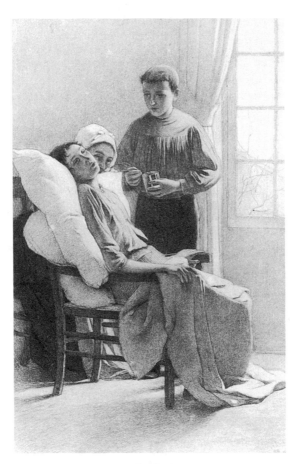

pathodixiac

There is almost nothing as irritating as this species of self-involved bore. **Pathodixiacs** abuse our sympathy, holding us hostage with their interminable tales of woe. No, we are not interested in your wheat allergy, thank you very much. If only muteness were one of your complaints, or deafness one of ours.

"After enduring months of listening to Lucille the **pathodixiac** complain about an illness they all knew to be imaginary, her coworkers decided to validate her and spiked her lunch with a hefty dose of salmonella." *(compare egrote)*

peccable /*PEK uh bul*/ adj • Liable to sin.
 [Latin *peccare* to sin]

peccable

How strange that the word *impeccable* (meaning in its first sense "not capable of sinning"), which applies to no one, should survive the test of time while the seemingly much more useful **peccable** has fallen by the linguistic wayside.   (*compare* **meable**)

pediculous /*ped IK yoo lus*/ adj • Afflicted with *pediculosis* (lice infestation); lousy.

"To the great distress of the other parents, Mrs. Willoughby insisted on continuing to send her **pediculous** children to school, insisting 'Lice are nothing, education is everything.'"

pediculous

peniculas /*pen IK yoo las*/ n • An undersized penis.

[Latin *peniculas* small penis]

The authors, being themselves male, feel an obligation to observe a certain code of honor and not make fun of other members of their gender for this most personal of shortcomings. That said, there is also an obligation to all readers to adequately present the most correct and specific form of opprobrium for each and every situation.

"Hampton had finally built up enough nerve to take out an ad in the Personals boldly stating that he was a SWM/**Peniculas,** but the letters of derision he received so outnumbered the inquisitive ones that he decided to give up dating forever."

(*compare* **brachyphallic, micropenis, subvirate**)

peotillomania /*pee o til o MAY nee uh*/ n • The neurotic habit of constantly pulling at one's penis.

"Although the years of **peotillomania** had been trying ones for both him and his family, Lucien was now the proud possessor of an organ the length of which would be the envy of many a mule." (*compare* **sacofricosis, trichotillomania**)

peotomy /*pee OT o mee*/ n • Amputation of the penis.

Though most male readers will probably skip quickly over this word, the authors have gone to the trouble of offering a sentence to illustrate this uncomfortably evocative term:

"In a vain attempt to keep his wife from leaving him for another woman, Adam decided to have the **peotomy.**"

(*compare* **skoptsy**)

perissotomist /*peh rih SOT o mist*/ n • A knife-happy surgeon.

We've all heard the horror stories: Someone enters a clinic to have a small growth removed and exits minus a rather large limb. Chalk another one up for the **perissotomist.**

(*compare* ***sangrado***)

petulcity /*pet OOL sit ee*/ n • Offensive forwardness.

This is the word to apply to the behavior of that singularly irritating sort of person who intrudes on everyone at one time or another: the kind who fifteen minutes after meeting you at a staid dinner party is asking you the most intimate questions about your love life (and worse still, offering vivid descriptions of his own). Try jabbing him in the thumb webbing with a salad fork; if your hosts are at all gracious, they will understand. (*compare* ***klazomaniac***)

phallalgia /*fal AL jee uh*/ n • Pain in the penis.

Everyone is familiar with the phrase "pain in the ass,"

petulcity

but one never hears "pain in the penis" used figuratively—whether because both sexes need a phrase they can identify with, or because it hits too close to home for men, it's hard to be sure.

"With his **phallalgia** increasing by the minute, Edsel bitterly cursed his brothers for dragging him to the bordello the night before."   (compare **pudendagra**)

phallocrypsis /fal o KRIP sis/ n • Retraction of the penis.

While this word is generally used in a medical sense, it can also describe that greatest of male fears: shrinkage.

"Percy's fondest dream turned into his worst nightmare when he went skinny-dipping with not one, not two, but three luscious young women, only to be dealt a whopping case of **phallocrypsis** by the icy water." (compare **shram**)

phalloplasty /FAL o plass tee/ n • Plastic surgery of the penis.

"Oh, how Wesley wished he had never accepted that dare; his penis was horribly twisted now, and no amount of **phalloplasty** could fully restore it." (compare **balanoplasty**)

phallorhiknosis /fal or hik NO sis/ n • The shrivelling of the penis with old age.

"Of all the indignities visited upon Philip in his later years—the balding, the bulging waistline, the growing incontinence—it was his **phallorhiknosis** that did the most to obliterate his sense of manhood."

(compare **obsolagnium**)

philodox /FAI lo dox/ n • A person in love with his own opinions.

Everybody has opinions. The **philodox,** however, is overly found of his or her own, and not fond enough of

phallorhiknosis

yours. The next time you encounter one of these insufferable people, it may cheer you slightly to know the proper word. (*compare* **sophomaniac**)

philopornist /*fie lo PORN ist*/ n • An afficionado of prostitutes.

"The mayor was an avid **philopornist,** much to the consternation of his aides, who seemed to spend most of their time either watching out for the cops or scheduling appointments at private health clinics." (*compare* **cypripareunia**)

philosophaster /*fil OSS o fast er*/ n • One who pretends to be knowledgeable about philosophy.

Philosophers have a long history of being hated by nearly everybody, including their own colleagues. Why, then, is the pejorative term **philosophaster** even necessary? Isn't "philosopher" a stinging enough insult in itself? One guess is that these miscreants came up with the term themselves to use in insulting one another. (*compare philodox*)

pica /*PIKE uh*/ n • Depraved appetite; hunger for such nonfoods as ashes, clay, starch, chalk, and plaster.

Pica has been observed in cases of pregnancy, nutrient deficiency, intestinal worms, and madness.

"The maternity-wear fashion shoot was delayed due to **pica** when the pregnant supermodel began compulsively stuffing her face with handfuls from the playground's sandbox."

pilgarlic /*pil GAR lik*/ n • A sorry-looking bald person.

There are seemingly dozens of words for bald, baldness, and bald people in the English language. All of them are too bloody boring for this book, except **pilgarlic**, which with its "peeled garlic" imagery does have a certain savoir faire.

pinchback /*PINCH back*/ n • Someone who is so miserly that he or she will not buy clothes.

"Fidel, incorrigible **pinchback** that he was, possessed but one pair of threadbare trousers, of indeterminate hue. When dining out, he would often pick up the check—then fling it down again and run into the men's room until someone else paid it." (*compare pinchgut*)

pinchgut /*PINCH gut*/ n • Someone who is so miserly that he or she will not buy food.

pilgarlic

"Growing up with a **pinchgut** for a father was a terrible chore. Whereas most families would order a pizza and eat it all at once, we had to eat the cheese and sauce off the top on the first day, and the following day we would get to eat the crust."   (*compare* **pinchback, swedge**)

pinchpin /*PINCH pin*/ n • A married woman insistent upon her sexual rights; one who demands sex from her husband.

"Prescott wouldn't have minded being married to a **pinchpin** had his newlywed's notion of her rights not included wearing leather and spikes to bed, which made him somewhat . . . well, uncomfortable."

pissburnt /PISS burnt/ adj • Stained with urine.

The thrifty reader is advised to remember the word **pissburnt** whenever he or she is tempted to drag home a "perfectly good, just slightly discolored" mattress that someone has put out on the sidewalk.

"Clayton was very much disgusted when the appraiser informed him that the centerpiece of his living room set, what he had believed to be an exquisite eighteenth-century damask settee, was actually a cheap loveseat, most likely manufactured in Eastern Europe, **pissburnt** and stained by the sun." *(compare bepiss, leint)*

pizzle /PIZZ ul/ n • The penis of a bull, or other large beast, especially when dried to a rubbery consistency and used either to flog people with or as a sexual aid.

Many other languages have similar terms for the penis of a bull, but **pizzle** is nonetheless a distinctly English word. For only the English include a **pizzle's** use as a whipping instrument with its general definition.

Nothing like a good **pizzle** after tea and crumpets, what?

"Despite the consequent rash of whippings, Alderman Wheal's approval ratings soared after he had the police batons replaced with **pizzles**." *(compare byental)*

pleionosis /PLAY o NO sis/ n • An exaggerated sense of one's own importance.

"After he lost his job to corporate downsizing, Dudley bought himself a cab. On his days off he would amuse himself by picking up only the most officious-looking businessmen at the airport and then intentionally getting stuck in traffic jams. It warmed the cockles of his heart to hear their squealing voices dripping with **pleionosis** in the back seat: 'You don't understand! I have a *very* important meeting to attend!' "   (*compare* **autotheist, cockalorum**)

pleonexia /*plee o NEX ee uh*/ n • Insane greed.

"The trick-or-treating children eventually learned not to ring the doorbell of Mr. Gifford, the stock trader, whose **pleonexia** was so great that instead of giving candy he often took it away."   (*compare* **oniomania**)

ploiter /*PLOY ter*/ v • To labor ineffectually.

A fine and memorable little word, suitable-sounding for its definition. **Ploiter** can be applied to amateurs and professionals alike, and to those who try hard at a given task as well as those whose hearts are just not in it.

"This year's convention of the United Gasket Changers' Union featured a full and varied agenda, headed by the keynote speech, "How Best to **Ploiter** for Your Union."

(*compare* **aidle, eyeservant**)

plooky /*PLOO kee*/ adj • Covered with pimples.

"The designer started a bold new trend in fashion advertising with his decision to hire only the **plookiest** adolescent models."   (*compare* **foveated**)

plorabunde /*PLORE uh bund*/ n • A person who weeps excessively.

"Her friends didn't understand how she could remain married to such a **plorabunde,** for Jasmine's husband would frequently spend half the night weeping quietly in bed. But she had long ago taught herself to cope by just lying there and pretending that she was asleep until it was over."   (*compare* **begrutten, rectopathic**)

plunderbund /PLUN *der bund*/ n • A thieving group of businessmen.

There are several terms in the English language for a thieving group of businessmen, such as *Democrats, Republicans,* and *network executives.* **Plunderbund** can be used interchangeably with any of these.

*(compare **malversation**)*

plutomaniac /PLOOT o MAY *nee ak*/ n • A person under the delusion that he or she is wealthy.

"Charlie Dawkins, **plutomaniac** and wino, would spend his entire welfare check on the first day, happily lying on a park bench and gorging on foie gras and Rhinish wine. The remainder of the month he subsisted on muscatel and canned sardines." *(compare **callomaniac, sophomaniac**)*

podobromhidrosis /po do brome hid RO sis/ n • Smelly feet.

"Reasoning that it was better to be an oddball than a pariah, Terry began dunking his feet in a tub of cologne before leaving the house each morning, so as to mask his chronic and incurable **podobromhidrosis**."

*(compare **bromidrosis, maschalephidrosis**)*

poger /POJ er/ n • A passive and older male homosexual.

"By day, it seemed a typical stodgy English public school. The crisp autumnal air resounded with the crack of cricket bats and with choruses of upper-class scions reciting Greek and Latin. But by night the school transformed itself into a pit of iniquity, with fresh-faced young students and hoary old professors alike engaging in lantern-lit bacchanals featuring unspeakable amusements, with the evening's proceedings often culminating in a frenzied ritual known as 'Roger the **Poger.**'" (*compare **ingler, sodomitess***)

pogogniasis /PO go NAI uh sis/ n • Growth of a beard on a woman.

"As head of public relations for the international poultry conglomerate, one of Chelsea's least favorite duties was to deny any link between the hormones used in the vast chicken plants and the persistent outbreaks of **pogogniasis** afflicting the Central American villagers."

On rainy days I'll reminisce
the pretty girls I've got to kiss.
And try to forget
the few I regret;
*the ones with **pogogniasis.***
(*compare **androgalactozemia, crurotrichosis***)

polakuiria /pol ok YOO ree uh/ n • An exceedingly frequent need to urinate.

A disorder seemingly confined to just two groups of people: those trying to fall asleep while lying comfortably in their beds, and small children in automobiles.
(*compare **micturition, nocturia***)

polymasthus /polly MASS thus/ n • A person with *polymastia*: more than the usual number of breasts or nipples.

"'Estelle wasn't just another dull **polymasthus**,' mused the old ex-carnival geek with a faint and somewhat rueful smile. 'She could really make a sideshow come alive.'"
(*compare **triorchid***)

porknell /PORK nell/ n • A person who resembles a fat pig.

"The raft was small, the water supply was running low,

and the last of the food had run out days ago. Jacob the **porknell** was beginning to feel distinctly uncomfortable with the hungry looks the other castaways were giving him." *(compare **blowmaunger, pursy**)*

pornocracy */pore NOK ruh see/* n • Government by whores.

This one comes with a little historical background. The term **pornocracy** was once used by the opponents of Pope Sergius III (A.D. 904–11), regarded as one of the worst and most profligate popes in history. Sergius had a notorious **parnel** named Marozia, who was widely resented for her great influence over the papal court. As a result, some referred to the regime as a **pornocracy**.

A member of a ruling **pornocracy** is called a *pornocrat*.

"Many of those polled said they would prefer a **pornocracy** to their current system, reasoning that at least the whores would be honest about their whoring."

*(compare **cypripareunia, pornophilist**)*

potvaliant */pot VAL ee ent/* adj • Bold or brave when drunk; more inclined to fight when inebriated.

This is the proper word for someone with the misplaced confidence that comes from being soused. When it's the whisky talking, it's also the *potvalor*: a phenomenon that encourages people to put their lives in danger, or at least to make complete asses of themselves.

"When he awoke the following afternoon, the last thing Pegram could remember was climbing aboard the honky-tonk's mechanical bull in a **potvaliant** frenzy."

*(compare **barlichood**)*

priapism */PRY up ism/* n • Painful, constant erection without sexual excitement.

potvaliant

"Mr. Cadwallader searched long and hard for a remedy for his **priapism**, but nothing seemed to work: not cold compresses, not thinking about his tubby aunt Lucinda, not even smacking himself with a steel ruler."

*(compare **chordee**)*

pricklouse /*PRIK louse*/ n • A pejorative term for a tailor.

Oh, what a supple and colorful language English is! What other tongue could so elegantly and contemptuously conjure up the image of a poor slob sewing away on a flea-infested pair of trousers?

proctalgia /*prok TAL jee uh*/ n • Pain in the anus or rectum.

"Grimacing in pain as she reached for the bathroom tissue, Vera wondered whether the triple-jalapeno omelet of the night before had been worth this attack of morning **proctalgia**." *(compare **pygalgia, rectalgia**)*

pronovalent /pro NO vuh lent/ n • Only able to have sex while lying down.

"In a desperate attempt to spice up their moribund sex life, the Wilsons tried hypnosis, acupuncture, and an adjustable bed, but Mr. Wilson's **pronovalence** simply could not be overcome." *(compare **stasivalence**)*

proxenetism /prok SEN it ism/ n • Pimping performed by a female.

"Nobody in the small town where she grew up would have guessed that Dorothy's much-vaunted matchmaking abilities at the penny socials would eventually lead her to the far more lucrative world of **proxenetism** in the big city." *(compare **dietairistriae**)*

psaphonic /saf ON ik/ adj • Seeking fame and glory for oneself.

In ancient Libya there lived a man named Psapho, who was clever enough to realize that most people will listen to a talking animal before they listen to another person. So he taught an enormous host of parrots to say the words "Psapho is a god" (see **autotheist**) and then set them free, after which he was worshipped by many of the locals. Thus this word was born.

"Oscar figured that if he could get a rumor going among the female students concerning his lovemaking prowess, he would have his pick of the campus nubiles. So he hit upon the **psaphonic** plan of scrawling anonymous complimentary messages about his sexual expertise—and equipment—on bathroom walls throughout the college. Unhappily for him, he did not possess the nerve to invade the *women's* bathrooms for this purpose, and so he ended up being dogged by the wrong kind of rumors."

psychrotic /*sai KROT ik*/ adj • Sexually frigid.

It is hard to say whether its similarity to *psychotic* helps this word or hurts it. Regardless, **psychrotic** is useful for alluding to what is an unfortunate condition.

(*compare **anorgasmic, dyspareunia***)

pudendagra /*poo DEN duh gruh*/ n • Pain in the genitals.

"Jasper's only pair of blue jeans were a little tight on him, and after one day at the dude ranch he came down with an incapacitating case of **pudendagra**."

(*compare **phallalgia***)

pursy /*PURSE ee*/ adj • Fat and short of breath.

"We on the hiking trip had grown weary of dragging the **pursy** Melissa along with us. Forever gobbling candy bars and begging for a rest, she was a nuisance to us all. On the third day we left her behind at daybreak, with half a canteen of water and two sticks of nougat."

(*compare **blowmaunger, porknell***)

pygalgia /*pig AL jee uh*/ n • Pain in the buttocks.

"Marty was getting his ass kicked so badly in Scrabble, it's a wonder he didn't put down the word **pygalgia**."

(*compare **proctalgia, rectalgia***)

pygobombe /*PIE go bom*/ n • A woman with big, sexy buttocks.

From the Greek *pyge* (buttocks) + *bombe* (rounded).

pudendagra

A lovely word. Why say "the bombshell with the bodacious bottom," when **pygobombe** is at your disposal?

*(compare **callipygian, steatopygous**)*

pygophilous */pie go FIL us/* adj • Fond of buttocks.

"To the mixed horror and amusement of the dinner party, Dean, our **pygophilous** adolescent cousin, began telling us all once again that if he were to be reincarnated, he sure hoped to come back as a chair."

*(compare **mazophilous**)*

pyriform */PIH rif orm/* adj • Pear-shaped.

Pyriform is certainly not the most depraved word in this lexicon. It is, however, perfect for describing a certain depressingly common male physical type: The out-of-shape man whose wide, generous middle tapers to very narrow shoulders.

"Not since the meteor shower had Judy been so forcefully reminded of the power of gravity as at the company picnic full of **pyriform** ad men."

*(compare **fabiform, myatonia**)*

quaestuary /*KWESS tyoo air ee*/ n • One who is interested only in profit.

"Dennis, the real-estate **quaestuary**, simply could not understand why anyone would criticize his decision to raze the orphanage to make way for yet another golf course. 'Come on,' he would say with great incredulity. 'Do you have any idea how much *money* we're talking about here?'"

(*compare* **barathrum, rabiator**)

quakebuttock /*KWAKE but uk*/ n • A trembling coward.

Some compound words, like **bedswerver, smell-smock,** and **quakebuttock,** are special because they convey their meaning by evoking a visual, fairly outrageous action that somehow embodies the spirit of the definition. These words are instantly memorized, and no one ever forgets what they mean. The real reason **quakebuttock** made this book, however, is that the authors were short on good words that start with the letter *q*. (*compare* **sterky**)

quibberdick /*KWIB er dik*/ n • A nasty quibbler.

The good thing about the word **quibberdick** is that people are not likely to mistake it for a compliment—even if they are not sure exactly what it means.

"Oh, how quickly the bloom came off the rose! Mona had only just begun to fall for the seemingly gallant Francesco when a petulant little incident over which movie to see revealed him to be a shrill and small-minded **quib-berdick.** Now he stood about as much chance of sharing her bed as a diseased porcupine."

(*compare **baratress, breedbate***)

· R ·

rabiator /RAY *bee ate or*/ n • A violent and greedy person.

"Of course it was just the luck of the draw, but the Sawyers couldn't help but feel a bit cheated. It didn't seem fair that some lucky family abroad was getting their angel of a son for nine months, while in exchange they had to provide room and board to an ill-tempered **rabiator** who threw terrible tantrums whenever his meals were less than huge, and who always had poppy seeds stuck between his orange teeth." (*compare **barathrum***)

rabulistic /*rab yoo* LIST *ik*/ adj • Characterized by legal trickery.

"It was a huge success on the mystery theater circuit, although everyone seemed to take *The Rabulistic Murders* for a feel-good comedy, perhaps because of the scene in which the drunken mob beat the three lawyers to death with their own briefcases." (*compare **barrator, leguleian***)

raddled /RAD *uld*/ adj • Aged and made worse by debauchery.

"The women at the ski lodge always looked forward to the yearly arrival of Sven, he of the drunken nocturnal romps in the snow. Alas, this year the aging lothario had grown so thoroughly **raddled** that the best he could come up with was a desultory pinch on the buttocks for most of them." *(compare **blowze, mulierose**)*

rammish /*RAM ish*/ adj • Strong-smelling, like a ram. Also, lustful, like a ram.

"I'm feeling rather **rammish,** dearie; would you mind terribly much favoring me with a sponge bath?"

*(compare **caprylic, hircine**)*

ranivorous /*ran IV or us*/ adj • Frog-eating.

Like *delicate, showy, and skittish,* **ranivorous** is one of those rare adjectives that one can apply to both storks and Frenchmen. *(compare **cepivorous, frenchified**)*

rantallion /*ran TAL ee un*/ n • A man or boy whose scrotum hangs lower than his penis.

Or, one "whose shot pouch is longer than the barrel of his piece."—Sir Francis Grose, *1811 Dictionary of the Vulgar Tongue*

recrudescence /*re crud ESS ence*/ n • The reappearance of a wound or sore; figuratively, the reappearance of something bad.

While the authors by no means wish to deprive the reader of the right to use the word **recrudescence** to describe those nasty sores that just won't go away, it is to be hoped that the word will play more of a figurative role in most vocabularies.

While romancing a winsome young doll,
my ex-wife just happened to call.
*This **recrudescence***
did cause my tumescence
to shrivel to nothing at all.

rectalgia /rek TAL jee uh/ n • Pain in the rectum.

Yes, there are a few words that mean "pain in the ass." But there are also so many different things in life deserving of this description. For your daily need to describe such pains (be they situations, coworkers, or anything else), you now have an array of options.

*(compare **proctalgia, pygalgia**)*

rectopathic /rek toe PATH ik/ adj • Easily hurt emotionally.

Rectopathic people are always fun to tease. Unless you are completely devoid of talent in this area, it should be possible to drive one to tears in under fifteen minutes.

"Exasperated from constantly walking on eggshells in the office, Jameson decided to hurt the feelings of his **rectopathic** executive assistant one last time, sacking him over the Christmas holidays."

*(compare **anaclitic, begrutten, plorabunde**)*

renifleur /ren uh FLIRRH/ n • A sexual deviant with an unnatural attraction to body odors, especially urine.

"Clyde was ordered to clean out the latrines for failing to grease his rifle; little did the sergeant know he was sentencing the **renifleur** to his own personal Eden."

*(compare **osphresiophilia**)*

retifism /RET if ism/ n • Foot fetishism.

So-called after the eighteenth-century French fetishist Retif de la Bretonne, who must be glowing with pride from beyond the grave now that his name has been forever linked to this particular sexual aberration. Ah, immortality!

"Felipe had managed to parlay his **retifism** into a nice little career, what with the paid appearances on daytime

rectopathic

talk shows; now that the ads in the back of the newspaper were starting to pay off, he could smell a winner."

(*compare* **pageism**)

retrocopulation /ret ro cop yoo LAY shun/ n • Copulation from behind. Also, copulation between partners facing away from each other in a back-to-back position, as with some animals.

"Stoltzfus tried to convince his scripture-quoting wife that **retrocopulation** was morally acceptable (after all, didn't most of God's creatures do it that way?), but she wouldn't hear of it." (*compare **retromingent***)

retromingent /*ret ro MINJ ent*/ adj • Urinating backward, as with some animals.

"George's horse-and-buggy service failed almost immediately after it became apparent that he had purchased a pair of **retromingent** animals."

(*compare **retrocopulation***)

rhinoplast /*RINE o plast*/ n • A person who has had rhinoplasty (plastic surgery of the nose).

Rhinoplasty is one hell of an ugly word for an operation that is supposed to beautify. The highly applicable **rhinoplast** is less common, but equally unappealing.

"Jane just couldn't stand yet another cocktail party full of smug and overdressed **rhinoplasts**—not with her own massive honker in full attendance." (*compare **conky***)

rhypophagous /*rye POFF uh gus*/ adj • Dung-eating.
This one comes from the Greek *rhypos* (filth).
(*compare **coprophagous, merdivorous, scatophagous, stercovorous***)

ripesuck /*RIPE suk*/ n • One who is easily bribed.
A fittingly revolting term for this concept.

"While all the other lobbyists worked the phones furiously, J.B. sipped his highball, unworried about the upcoming vote. Good thing his long experience in Washington had taught him how to spot a **ripesuck** at sixty yards."

(*compare **boodler, cacique***)

rhinoplast

ructuosity /*ruk choo OSS it ee*/ n • Frequent belching.

    "It started with a bunch of brewery workers belching in unison to make the time pass quickly on the assembly line. Now they sold out such venues as Carnegie Hall. But the Milwaukee **Ructuosity** Choir never let their success go to their heads."   (*compare* ***fumosities***)

ripesuck

rudesby /*ROODS bee*/ n • A loud boor; a generally offensive person.

The **rudesby** is not on many people's endangered species list. In fact, it often seems that this offensive creature is more common today than at any other time in history.

It has certainly never been more *fashionable* to be a **rudesby.** Hallmarks of this pest include a liking for brutish and vulgar forms of entertainment; vapid and profane speech; vicious pets; monstrous vehicles; and clownish attire.

In any case, **rudesby** is a memorable and useful word, and most people will understand what it means at once, even if they are hearing it for the first time.

"Brett did not consider himself to be a **rudesby.** Blasting rap music from his SUV's outward-facing speakers late at night in residential districts was for him a sacred form of self-expression."

· S ·

sacofricosis /*sak o frik O sis*/ n • Habitual rubbing of the genitals through one's pant pocket.

Call it pocket pool, or what you will; even if it is not habitual, every man is prone to a little **sacofricosis** on occasion. Sometimes it is a persistent itch he absolutely must scratch; sometimes a slight adjustment is unavoidable; on occasion he may simply need reassurance that he's still all there. And pockets are so conveniently located, just crying out to be utilized to their full potential.

"Busted during a particularly indelicate flurry of **sacofricosis,** Boyle tried to save face by making a big show of searching for his keys." (*compare chiromania*)

sangrado /*san GRAH du*/ n • A quack; a medical impostor.

The next time you come down with a malady that is *iatrogenic* (caused by doctors), counter your physician's impenetrable jargon by giving him a little honorific of your own. (*compare perissotomist*)

saprostomus /*sup ROSS tuh muss*/ n • A person with bad breath.

Pity the **saprostomus,** for though he makes others choke, he himself suffers ostracization, and he knows not why. From the Greek *sapros* (putrid) + *stoma* (mouth).

"'Why didn't you tell me before?' cried Jim the **saprostomus** between sobs, as his friends and family brought their bad-breath intervention to a climax."

(compare **bromopnea**)

satyriasis /*sat ih RYE uh sis*/ n • Maniacal lustfulness in males.

This condition is named after those horny capripedes the *satyrs,* perpetually erect goat-men of ancient myth.

(compare **contrectation, erotomania, lascivia, tentigo**)

saulie /*SAW lee*/ n • A hired mourner at a funeral.

Oh, humanity.

"First the expense of the undertaker's bill, then the marble tomb, now the **saulies** holding out for more money; Eidelfilch's widow thanked the Lord that her husband, while unpopular, had at least been stinking rich."

(compare **claqueur**)

scaff /*SKAFF*/ v • To beg for food in a contemptible fashion.

Scaff invites comparison with the word **groak,** meaning "to stare silently at someone while they are eating, in the hope that they will offer some food," although **scaffing** takes things a step further. At least the **groaker** maintains a semi-dignified posture while **groaking**; not so the **scaffer.**

"It was always the same thing with the little animals, whenever Ahmed brought food home. The whining, the drooling, the pawing at his clothes—all making it impossible for him to eat in peace. When was his brood of small children ever going to stop **scaffing** and learn to forage on their own?"

(compare **lickspigot**)

scambler /SKAM blur/ n • One who drops in uninvited at dinner time in the hope of getting free food.

"An inveterate **scambler,** Otis knew who ate early and who dined late; and he ate so fast that when he was on his game he could usually **scamble** at least three dinners in one day." (*compare* **groak, smellfeast**)

scaphism /SKAFF ism/ n • The practice of covering a victim in honey and strapping him to a hollow tree exposed to stinging insects, in order to inflict a lingering death.

"Ferdinand was an excellent torturer, and a tireless self-promoter as well; just that morning he had sent placards to all the local inquisitors reading "Thumbscrews not working? Why not give **scaphism** a try? Affordable rates. Group discounts.' " (*compare* **bastinado, ganch**)

scatophage /SKAT o faj/ n • An eater of excrement.

Other words for this include **merdivore** and **coprophagist.**

"When Eunice found out that halitosis was to blame, she breathed a sigh of relief, for in her heart of hearts she had always harbored the suspicion that her husband was a closet **scatophage.**"

scatophagous /skat OFF uh gus/ adj • Feeding on excrement.
(*compare* **coprophagous, merdivorous, rhypophagous, stercovorous**)

scaurous /SKOW russ/ adj • Having thick ankles.

"How all the girls hated the winsome Belinda. She was the prettiest girl at school, and all the boys longingly followed her with their eyes in the hallways between classes. When in the locker room one day the discovery was made that she was extraordinarily **scaurous**—and insecure about it—they leapt on this vulnerability like jackals on a still-born antelope."

scombroid /SKOM broid/ adj • Resembling a mackerel.

One of the odder words in the singularly descriptive and comprehensive language we call English. Few people have used it; fewer still to describe something without gills. Still, the reader is urged to commit it to memory. For who knows? One day the occasion may very well arise to insult a sallow, saucer-eyed, chinless, thick-lipped runt of a fellow. In this case, no other term will do.

scopophilia /skope uh FIL ee uh/ n • Sexual interest in erotic imagery, especially when used as a substitute for actual sex.

"Being struck suddenly blind would have taxed any man, but for Mr. Bigelow, with his acute **scopophilia,** it smacked of divine vengeance."

scoracrasia /skore uh KRAY zhuh/ n • Involuntary defecation.

"Wedding jitters? Maybe. Whatever the cause, Jill's pre-nuptial **scoracrasia** was rapidly becoming cause for alarm."
(compare **copracrasia, encopresis**)

scrag /SKRAG/ n • A lean and bony person.

There is a glut of words for fat people in the English language. Terms for their skinny counterparts are sorely needed in order to provide some semblance of balance, especially today, with images of pouting, glamorized **scrags** festooning every billboard and magazine cover within eye-

scopophilia

shot. Unfairly, such words are relatively few and far between, so make the most of **scrag.**

"'You can never be too rich or too thin,' the unhappy little **scrag** said to herself, washing down her guilty feast of half a rice cake and a stalk of celery with a diet protein drink on her way home from aerobics class."

(*compare* **chichiface, gammerstang**)

screable /*SKREE uh bl*/ adj • Which may be spit upon.

Every so often a city or municipality will wage some

scrag

sort of public campaign exhorting its citizens to not spit so much, or to not spit on the sidewalk. While these efforts are laudable, they really don't go far enough. Certainly sidewalks should not be the recipient of all this expectoration, at least not when there are so many **screable** people to go around. Indeed, life abounds with people who deserve to be spit on. So the next time you hawk and clear a gob of phlegm from your throat, hold on to it for a while; chances are it will not be long before your eye settles upon some eminently **screable** individual.

*(compare **bespawled, sialismus**)*

screation /*skree AY shun*/ n • Neurotic and excessive hawking and clearing of the throat.

"Following as it did his weekly act of **irrumation,** Comstock's wife's prolonged **screation** did little to enhance his blissful afterglow."

screeve /*SKREEV*/ n • A begging letter. v • To write begging letters.

A writer of begging letters is known as a **screever.**

"Soaring tuition and a renewed emphasis on practical education led the small progressive college to require all incoming freshmen to take **Screeving** 101 in addition to algebra and a foreign language. Instead of a term paper, students had to convince their parents to wire them one thousand dollars to cover a fictional medical emergency."

*(compare **cadator, mumblecrust**)*

scybalous /*SIB il us*/ adj • Resembling small, hardened chunks of feces that can form in a diseased colon (*scybala*).

Sure, this is an obscure medical term that nobody will understand should you whip it out in an argument, but who cares? Off the top of one's head, one would be hard-pressed to think of a more offensive thing to say to someone than that they resemble a small and hardened fecal mass lodged inside a diseased internal organ. *(compare **coproma**)*

seeksorrow /*SEEK sorrow*/ n • One who seeks to give himself vexation.

This word applies to everybody at one time or another. For reasons that are hard to understand, we do such things as venture to the mall the day after Thanksgiving, try to fix our own plumbing, and become fans of losing sports teams (as well as fall in love, have babies, and go on family vacations).

shardborn /*SHARD born*/ adj • Born or residing in excrement.

"How long would the greatest political mistake of his career keep coming back to haunt him? After all, it was decades ago that he had made the infamous comment about the '**shardborn** Okies.'" (*compare* **fimiculous**)

sharny /*SHAR nee*/ adj • Befouled with dung.

It is one of the great mysteries of the English language: Why do we have so many words for spraying (or getting sprayed) with shit? Does it actually happen that often? Or did the lexicographers of yesteryear amuse themselves by seeing who could come up with the best word for this horrid idea?

At last count there seemed to be at least a dozen such words. In the interest of scholastic thoroughness, the authors have included the seven they found most interesting: **beray, bescumber, conskite, immerd, ordured, sharny,** and **shitten.**

"Kelly was all for celebrating his ethnic heritage, but when it came to kissing the **Sharny** Stone, he balked."

(*compare* **ordured, shitten**)

shilpit /*SHILL pit*/ adj • 1) Feeble, puny, or sickly. 2) Weak, good-for-nothing, or watered-down.

With its various definitions, all clustering around the notion of worthless, **shilpit** is a good meat-and-potatoes type of general insult. Happily for us all, it can be used to describe just about anything....

*There was once a **shilpit** man*
*living in a **shilpit** house.*
*He drove a **shilpit** car*
*and wed a **shilpit** spouse.*
*He had a **shilpit** job*
to which he had to go.
*And sipped a **shilpit** beer*
*watching a **shilpit** show.*   (*compare **imbonity***)

shitten /SHIT en/ adj • Covered with or stained by feces.

"Meredith hated to make a fuss, but when her clothes came back **shitten** a second time, she resolved to have a word with the lady at the laundromat."

(*compare **beray, bescumber, conskite,***
immerd, ordured, sharny)

shotclog /SHOT klog/ n • An unpleasant drinking companion, tolerated only because he or she is buying the drinks.

(This particular form of generosity will absolve many sins.)

"As a **shotclog** par excellence, Woodrow was able to transform his inheritance into a form of social acceptance, at least among the circle of alcoholic artists who despised him, yet whose company he preferred."

(*compare **spunger***)

shram /SHRAM/ v • To shrivel or become numb from cold.

"As a movie star, Desmond's vanity knew no bounds, and he would have been tickled pink by the nude photos flooding the Internet had they not been taken when he was so unflatteringly **shrammed** from swimming."

(*compare **phallocrypsis***)

sialismus /*sai uh LIZ muss*/ n • An excessive flow of saliva.

The problem with people afflicted with **sialismus** is not just that they have too much spit in their mouths. It is the fact that they often seem to be hell-bent on sharing it with the world when they talk. Nobody loves a spitter. Not even his own mother.

"As a rock-star wannabe with a death wish, Henderson secretly felt that choking on his own vomit—as so many of his musical idols had done before him—would be 'a good way to go out.' He almost, but not quite, got his wish when his **sialismus** caused him to drown painlessly in his own spittle while sleeping one night."

(*compare **bespawled, screable***)

sialoquent /*sigh AL o kwent*/ adj • Apt to spray saliva when speaking.

One can always "compliment" a blustering or pompous speaker by referring to him as extremely **sialoquent**.

"All the the other seats were taken, so Amanda had no choice but to sit front and center, grit her teeth, and endure two hours of dehumanizing misting from Mr. Fletcher, the **sialoquent** history professor."

(*compare **conspue, sputative***)

skimmington /*SKIM ing ton*/ n • A ceremony in which a man whose wife beat him or cheated on him was publicly ridiculed.

The **skimmington** had its heyday in English villages several hundred years ago. However one feels about the social climate of that time and place, one must admit those English villagers possessed a real sense of community.

"It was ratings month again, and just like clockwork all the daytime talk shows put their best foot forward: nothing but big breasts and surprise **skimmingtons** would grace the airwaves for the next four weeks."

(*compare* **legruita, wetewold**)

skoptsy /*SKOPT zee*/ n, pl • An eighteenth-century breakaway Russian religious sect whose members castrated themselves out of an extreme devotion to sexual abstinence.

That must have taken a lot of balls. (*compare* **peotomy**)

slockster /*SLOK ster*/ n • One who entices away another's servants.

Slockster is one of those words that provide a notion of how people lived in the past. Because formerly the issue of stealing away servants must have been an important one, or there would have been no need for such a word. Then, as now, good help was probably hard to find. Today most people don't have servants, but a kind of **slockster** is common enough in other areas of the labor market, such as professional sports.

"Judge Hobarth had made a lot of enemies upholding the law. When the time came for his reelection, vicious rumors of mysterious origin began to circulate—how he was an atheist, a drunk, and a **slockster**."

slotterhodge /*SLOT er hoj*/ n • A messy eater.

"It was always an ordeal dining with Mr. and Mrs. **Slotterhodge,** and their gross corpulence only made their

slotterhodge

contemptible manners less excusable. Dribbling gravy from
their chins, leaning over one's plate with their mouths full,
and asking hopefully, 'You using that drumstick?' they
made me want to vomit." (*compare* **gundygut**)

slubberdegullion */slub er dee GULL yun/* n • A contemptible slob.

"Mr. Roth had a normal—if slightly dishevelled—appearance, and if it weren't for the odor of spoiled milk that
followed him everywhere, no one would have guessed that
at home he was a complete **slubberdegullion**."

smatchet */SMACH it/* n • A small and nasty person.

"Bridget hated the game of spin the bottle; whenever her
turn came around, the bottle would invariably come to rest
pointing directly at Billy, the **smatchet** with the bad teeth."

smegma /SMEG muh/ n • A cheesy, foul-smelling material found under the foreskin of the penis and near the clitoris. From the Greek *smegma* (soap).

Smegma is one of the better-known words in this lexicon. It also happens to be one of the more disgusting.

smeke /SMEEK/ v • To go too far in one's flattery.

"Ingratiating small talk was Casey's specialty. But as soon as the words were out of his mouth, he realized he had **smeked** badly by referring in passing to his host's 'beautiful daughter.' In reality, the girl in question strongly resembled a monkey on the Nature Channel. The question was, could he backtrack without making things worse?"

(*compare* **fart-sucker, subsycophant**)

smellfeast /SMELL feast/ n • A mealtime moocher.

"It was squat and fat, with nostrils big enough to fit both thumbs, but to Ludwig the **smellfeast** his nose was his greatest asset." (*compare* **scambler**)

smellsmock /SMELL smock/ n • A revolting lecher.

"When the news came out about Mr. Wilburn, Janet couldn't believe that the kindly old pushbroom who always opened the door for her was actually an inveterate **smellsmock** who exposed himself to schoolgirls."

sneckdraw /SNEK draw/ n • One who stealthily enters a house; a thief. Hence, any sly, crafty person.

"All the campers were supposed to go to the lake for swimming lessons, but Ferdinand, the eight-year-old **sneckdraw,** had other ideas. Backtracking to the cabins on tiptoe, he made directly for the bunks of those children who had received care packages, and spent the next hour gorging on all manner of candy. He then he wet his hair, grabbed his towel, and hid along the path to fall in step with the returning troop." (*compare **snudge***)

snivelard /*SNIV uh lard*/ n • Someone who speaks through the nose; a whiny person.

With its similarity to *sniveler,* **snivelard** certainly has a contemptible cast to it. It is another example (see **clatterfart**) of a very insulting-looking word that has an only slightly insulting definition. Such words are useful when one wishes to heap scorn upon someone but lacks better ammunition. Some pretty good insults can be formed thusly, such as "I am not in the habit of arguing with **snivelards.** And you, sir, are a **snivelard.**"

"The smarmy and repugnant little **snivelard** at the Help Desk so offended Marcie that when he turned his back for a moment she struck him in his bald spot with the courtesy phone, then acted like nothing had happened as he whined through his nose in pain."

snollygoster /*SNOLL ee GOSS ter*/ n • An unprincipled person, especially a politician.

"Ethan knew that his opponent didn't really have sex with pigs, but he also knew that it would steal momentum from his campaign if he had to take time out to deny the rumor. And before anyone could squeal foul, the young **snollygoster** had won his third consecutive term as president of the high school debating society."

(*compare **boodler, empleomaniac, malversation, ripesuck***)

snool /*SNOOL*/ v • To depress someone by constantly chiding or nagging him or her.

snool

"Three days into the vacation with his wife, two children, and sister-in-law, Artie was so thoroughly **snooled** that he could do little more than hunker in the back of the camper, sobbing quietly into his can of Dinty Moore."

snoutband /*SNOUT band*/ n • One who constantly interrupts his or her companions in order to contradict them.

"Goddard tried ignoring him, spilling his drink on him, even farting in his general direction. Nothing, however, but nothing would deter the cursed little **snoutband** seated to his right at the dinner party, the one torpedoing every one of his attempts to make a good impression with the ladies by contradicting all of his carefully constructed lies."

snudge /SNUJ/ n • A scoundrel who hides under the bed, waiting for a chance to rob the house.

"Patience was the key to Wolfgang's status as a world-class **snudge.** Of course, it also helped to have a slender physique and a bladder several times normal size."

(*compare* **sneckdraw**)

snurt /SNURT/ v • To eject mucus from the nose when sneezing. "A bright child, Granville might have had a promising future in life, had he not **snurted** on the class bully that grim day while in line at the lunch counter."

(*compare* **meldrop**)

sodomitess /sod o mit ESS/ n • A female sodomite, in the passive sense.

A thievish stockbroker named Mel
was housed with an inmate from Hell.
*No **sodomitess***
e'er felt such distress
as he felt every night in his cell. (*compare* **ingler, poger**)

sophomania /soff o MAY nee uh/ n • The delusion that one is wise.

An unattractive and widespread condition that does not discriminate on the basis of race, class, color, or creed; some degree of which has bewitched everyone from the guy on the bus filling in the Wonderword to the inventor of colored cling wrap. (*compare* **witling**)

sophomaniac /*soff o MAY nee ak*/ n • One under the delusion that he or she is wise.

Sophomania is a common and deeply irritating condition that can crop up in any type of person. It is especially rife, however, among those with a little too much education. A word to the (genuinely) wise: Don't waste your time arguing with **sophomaniacs.** It is far better to ignore them completely, or poke them in the eye.

(*compare* **callomaniac, philosophaster, plutomaniac**)

sordes /*sore DEES*/ n, pl • Filthy, dark deposits that accumulate on the teeth and lips, consisting of foul, dried stomach secretions.

Yet another revolting medical term you probably had no idea existed. Isn't your life a little bit richer for the thought that someday you might wind up in a hospital bed with a tube up your nose and **sordes** on your lips?

sorn /*SORN*/ v • To sponge off of friends for room and board.

Some people are born to **sorn;** therein lies their greatest talent.   (*compare* **inkle**)

sorner /*SORE ner*/ n • One who sorns; one who imposes on the hospitality of another for room and board.

Originally, **sorner** was a legal term, referring to a type of criminal miscreant who procured food or lodging for himself through the use of force or menace. Now it applies to miscreants who take advantage of their friends.

"Basil changed his locks and his phone number when he learned his apartment had been given a three-star rating in *The Sorner's Guide to New York City.*"

(*compare* **scambler, smellfeast**)

spermatorrhea /*SPUR mat o REE uh*/ n • The abnormal leaking of semen through the penis without orgasm.

"Chadwick had taken to masturbating five or six times a day, hoping to rid himself of enough sperm to get out of wearing the diapers that had been prescribed for his severe **spermatorrhea.**" (*compare **aspermia, spermatoschesis***)

spermatoschesis /*SPUR mat o SKEE sis*/ n • The suppression of ejaculation.

It is difficult for most men to imagine **spermatoschesis** unnaccompanied by some sort of acute pain.

"Molesworth had always prided himself on his powers of **spermatoschesis**—and rightfully so—but on this most inopportune of occasions it had failed him."

(*compare **aspermia, spermatorrhea***)

spintry /*SPIN tree*/ n • A male prostitute.

Considering how many different words for *female* prostitute one has to wade through during a typical hour of dictionary-reading, it is a blatant injustice that there are not more words like **spintry** (for more on this, see **franion**).

"The jobless lexicographer reached for a pencil when he read this ad in the Help Wanted section: 'Wanted: **Spintry.** Excellent pay, benefits. Must have experience, references. Flexible hours.' Alas, he had no references."

(*compare **gugusse, gunsel, urning***)

spoffokins /*SPOFF uh kins*/ n • A prostitute posing as a wife.

"It was a slow night at the No-Tell Motel: just a couple of **spoffokins** and their bashful johns."

(*compare **parnel***)

sporge /SPORJ/ v • To be afflicted with diarrhea.

Seen on the page, the word **sporge** looks like it could mean just about anything, from the sound of a bouncing rubber ball to one of the ingredients in a mesclun salad. What a pleasant surprise to find that it actually means to be afflicted with the runs.

INSTRUCTIVE RHYME FOUND SCRAWLED INSIDE A PORT-O-POTTY AT THE ANNUAL GASTROENDOCRINOLOGISTS' CLAMBAKE:

If on shellfish we gorge,
*Then soon we will **sporge**.*

(*compare **imbulbitate, sterky***)

spraints /SPRAINTS/ n, pl • Otter feces.

An odd but memorable word. The challenge, of course, is to somehow work it into everyday conversation without sounding strained. Good luck.

"Charlie got a sprained elbow from constantly skimming the **spraints** from his swimming pool after a family of endangered otters took up residence there."

spuddle /SPUD l/ v • To attend to trifling matters as though they were of the greatest importance.

As a derisive term to describe the overofficious behavior of self-important people, **spuddle** is invaluable. In fact, anyone who has ever held a job should be familiar with the **spuddler.** Career advancement is often bestowed upon those employees who can **spuddle** more convincingly than their coworkers.

"No one had the heart to mock Haverford, the consumptive little office boy, for adopting a ludicrous aura of solemnity every time he doled out the new vials of correction fluid to the staff. Apparently, **spuddling** afforded the poor sod his main satisfaction in life." (*compare* **beadledom**)

spunger /*SPUN jer*/ n • One who drinks at the expense of another.

This is the flip side of a **shotclog**. We have all known **spungers**. Many of us have even aspired to be one.

Especially as they are pronounced the same, the reader might well ask what is the real difference between a **spunger** with a "u" and the familiar *sponger* with an "o." Well, this particular spelling also seems to go along with a more specific definition, at least according to Thomas Wright's *Dictionary of Obsolete and Provincial English* of 1857.

"Who came out ahead? It was hard to say. The friendless and socially inept tavern owner footed the bill for round after round of whiskeys, but the pathetic **spungers** gathered around him at the end of the bar had to pretend to enjoy his company, and to be interested in his endless stories that went nowhere. It was a sad situation all around."

(*compare* **shotclog**)

sputative /*SPEW tuh tiv*/ adj • Prone to spitting; liable to spit.

One of a mere handful of words in the English language that apply in equal measure to llamas and baseball players.

(*compare* **conspue, sialoquent**)

stasivalence /*stuh SIV uh lence*/ n • The state of only being able to have sex while standing.

"Clark's **stasivalence** was so pronounced, and his wife so much taller than he, that he often found himself in the embarrassing position of wearing high heels during love play." (*compare* **pronovalent**)

steatopygous /stee at OP ig us/ adj • Fat-assed.

Scattered throughout this book are words like **steato-pygous**, which are useful in those situations when one wishes to make crass comments about the anatomy of members of the opposite sex without risking being understood by the wrong person. Just remember to familiarize your friends with these words beforehand, to avoid the awkwardness of having to define them on the spot. Then you can speak freely in an impenetrable code.

(compare *callipygian, dasypygal*)

steatorrhea /stee at o REE uh/ n • Frothy, stinking excrement that floats, due to an abnormally high fat content.

Steatorrhea is also pale, greasy, and hard to flush. (This shit is really disgusting.)   (compare *allochezia, lientery*)

stercoraceous /STIR kuh RAY shuss/ adj • Of or pertaining to dung.   (compare *fecaloid, ordurous*)

stercorary /STIR kuh rare ee/ n • A place for storing dung.

"Mrs. Swinton was hardly a meddlesome landlady, but when one of her tenants decided to rent out his spare room as a **stercorary** for local farmers, she felt it was time to put her foot down."   (compare *urinarium*)

stercoverous /ster KOV er us/ adj • Dung-eating.

"We were all fond of the Henderson's dog—he was an affable pooch—but he had the disagreeable combination of being both insatiably **stercovorous** and inclined to lick one's face."   (compare *coprophagous, merdivorous, rhypophagous, scatophagous*)

sterky /STIR kee/ adj • Loose in the bowels from fear.

Some people have a tendency to get **sterky** in sticky

situations. Perhaps it is a vestige from some primeval defense mechanism—befouling oneself as a last resort to avoid the jaws of the lion.

" 'Are you *sure* everything's all right in there, sir?' F.W.'s executive assistant asked worriedly, knocking again on the bolted bathroom door. The stockholders in the crowded meeting hall were getting restless while their **sterky** CEO cowered on the toilet, terrified of having to answer publicly for the bad quarterly report."

Said the doelike young man from Turkey,
whose walk was alarmingly jerky,
"It's not that I'm lame
enfeebled or game,
*it's just that I'm constantly **sterky**."*

(*compare **ankyloproctia, imbulbitate***)

sthenolagnia /*sthen uh* LAG *nee uh*/ n • Sexual excitement in a woman arising from a display of strength or prowess.

"When Sally pushed him off the bed and barked 'Gimme twenty,' Hal realized that dating a girl with **sthenolagnia** was a lot like boot camp."

stinkard /*STINK ard*/ n • One who stinks.

A very special word for a very special person: he who stinks. Some **stinkards** are unaware of their stench, of course. Others just don't care.

"Finding work for Marcus, a confirmed **stinkard** who had prioritized his right not to bathe, was proving to be a bit of a challenge for the folks at the employment agency. Having no openings for lighthouse-keepers, they finally got him a job as night watchman at the town dump."

(*compare **ablutophobic, diamerdis, muscod, odorivector***)

stomatomenia /STO *mat o* MEE *nee uh*/ n • Bleeding from the mouth during menstruation.

The only solace for those readers traumatized by the definition of **stomatomenia** (and it is completely awful) is that the blood flow in question is not, obviously, redirected from the uterus. It is a separate, but simultaneous, flow of blood.

"While it pained Abigail immensely to cancel her date with the handsome Mr. Gladstone, she simply couldn't go out—not with her **stomatomenia** as bad as it was."

(*compare* ***bromomenorrhea***)

strene /STREEN/ v • To copulate; said of a dog.

With its uncomfortable similarity to *strain*, **strene** is not much more genteel-sounding than the phrase *doggy-style*. But it does have the benefit of being obtuse.

"Mr. and Mrs. Bullinger thought they had finally found a young couple willing to buy their split-level ranch, which they had been trying to sell for years. Things got off on the wrong foot the day of the house tour, however, when the neighbor's bulldog happened to be **strening** with a verminous mongrel in the front yard just as the prospective buyers arrived." (*compare* ***amplexus, fream***)

subsycophant /*sub* SIK *o fant*/ n • A revolting parasite.

"The angels couldn't decide in what form to reincarnate Sasha, for in life he had been such a revolting **subsycophant** that sending him back as a worm was too good for him. Finally, they elected to have him spend his next life as a blow-up sex doll, with the words 'up to 350 lbs. pressure' stamped on his left ankle."

(*compare* ***bdelloid, fart-sucker, lickspigot***)

subvirate /*SUB vih rate*/ n • One whose manhood is imperfect or undeveloped.

Subvirate is one of those delightfully descriptive words that are always handy to have around.

"Ettiene saw no reason why women, with their push-up bras and the like, should be the only ones to feel better about themselves by way of wearing an uncomfortable contraption. And so he fashioned a codpiece of sorts out of latex and foam, and marketed it to **subvirates** with a taste for tight clothing." (*compare **badling, nullimitus, peniculas***)

suggilate /*SUG il ate*/ v • To beat black and blue.

A whole phrase in one word. **Suggilate** is more specific and evocative than everyday words like *thrash, batter,* and

suggilate

pummel. Plus, it just sounds like it has punch. Saying you'd like to **suggilate** someone is a satisfying way to express your feelings of aggression and hostility.   (*compare* **fustigate**)

suoid /*SYOO oid*/ adj • Hoglike.

Suoid is different from the better-known *porcine* (piglike) in that it refers to *hogs*: bigger, fatter, and greedier than plain old pigs.

"Dexter didn't know if the two were connected, but after the surgery left him with a heart valve from a pig, he caught himself making love with distinctly **suoid** sqealings and gruntings."   (*compare* **blattoid**)

suppalpation /*sup pal PAY shun*/ n • The act of winning by fondling. Also, wheedling or coaxing.

In other words, stroking one's way to success.

   (*compare* **contrectation**)

surd /*SURD*/ n • A foolish and insensitive person.

[Latin *surdus* silent, mute, dumb]

"Finding that his new schoolmates already had a class bully and a class clown, Donahue took the bold step of combining the two roles, and as the class **surd** he would

suoid

stomp about making farting noises while he tormented the smaller children." *(compare **witling**)*

swartwouter /*SWART wow ter*/ n • A fleeing embezzler.

"Police searched the city in vain for Manfredy, the wily **swartwouter,** but he was already halfway across the Atlantic with a tote bag full of junk bonds, chuckling softly to himself over his second Mai Tai." *(compare **boodler**)*

swedge /*SWEJ*/ v • To leave without paying one's bill.
Quoth the sallow young man from New York
as he gorged on milkshakes and pork,
*"I find when I **swedge***
that it gives me an edge
if I first stab the host with a fork." *(compare **thrimmel**)*

symphoric /*sim FORE ik*/ adj • Accident prone.

"They had the patience of a dozen Jobs, the Butlers did, but eventually they grew tired of having to constantly safeguard their house after their **symphoric** son hit his teen years. With dreams of childless vacations and savings on college bills dancing through their heads, they began leaving metal forks near electrical outlets and investing in furniture with pointy edges." *(compare **looby**)*

syndyasmian /*sin die AZ mee an*/ adj • Pertaining to promiscuous sexual pairing, or to the temporary cohabitation of couples.

Finally, a word of dignity and charm with which to describe that much-maligned event: the one-night stand.

"No one in his family ever mentioned that dark day when Mr. Bradley quit his job, sold the car, and ran off to join a **syndyasmian** cult in California."

synechthry /*SIN ek three*/ n • The state of living together in enmity.

Yes, it has a daunting spelling, and frankly the authors are not absolutely sure how to pronounce it. But simply knowing that there is a word out there that encapsulates this all-too-common situation is worth something, isn't it?

"Insisting that they were staying together 'for the children's sake,' the Dorchesters spent twenty-five years gritting their teeth at each other in **synechthry** and raised a fine brood, all of whom eventually graduated to loveless marriages of their own."   (*compare cagamosis*)

·T·

tarassis /*tuh RASS iss*/ n • Male hysteria.

A curiously broad definition; perhaps even a little vague. For a mania that might fall under this heading, and one potential cause of **tarassis,** check the entry for **micromania.**

tartuffe /*tar TOOF*/ n • A religious hypocrite; one who affects piety.

[From the title character of a play by Molière]

A word like **tartuffe** presents a pleasing dilemma: namely, with such a wealth of potential targets at one's disposal, to whom does one apply the term? To the televangelist who rants against homosexuality while indulging in a wide variety of sexual pecadilloes? To the married congressman who professes a great love of the Scriptures, and meanwhile boinks a series of twenty-something aides? Yes! **Tartuffe** is an equal-opportunity word and should be employed liberally to describe all manner of religious hypocrites.

"Life at Sunday school had not been pleasant for young Linus; Father William in particular seemed to have it in for the young scamp. Then came that glorious day when he caught the wizened old **tartuffe** in a compromising position while frolicking in the holy water. In exchange for his

tartuffe

silence, Linus got to drink as much of the sacred wine as he wanted and sleep in the back pews during mass."

(*compare **antinomian, eisegetical***)

tenesmus /*ten EZ mus*/ n • Painful, spasmodic attempts to urinate or defecate, accompanied by involuntary straining.

It's that bit about "involuntary straining" that makes **tenesmus** uniquely unpleasant to contemplate.

"Grace felt nothing but sympathy for her husband during his racking bout with **tenesmus,** but she had to admit that the constant straining had helped him work off more than a few unnecessary pounds." (*compare **nisus***)

tentigo /*ten TIE go*/ n • Excessive lust; inordinate desire for sex.

Not to be confused with *impetigo,* a rash you get at the beach, although both conditions can be discomfiting for a man in a tight bathing suit.

(*compare **erotomania, lascivia, satyriasis***)

testiculous /*tess TIK yoo luss*/ adj • Having exceedingly large testicles.

[Latin *testiculus* testicle]

Certainly this word can be employed as a compliment, but it also has other uses. For instance, who hasn't at one time or another been treated to the grotesque but strangely riveting spectacle of some prim matron walking an enormous, **testiculous** dog down the street?

"No sultan of Siam ever sired more offspring than Gilbert, the **testiculous** milkman, whose forty-nine-year career spanned the man shortages of two world wars."

(*compare **macromaniac***)

thelypthoric /thel ip THOR ik/ adj • Morally corruptive to women.

A fairly cryptic definition; the authors wish their sources could be a bit more specific.

"As a young man and budding debaucher of women, Stanley had decided to make a study of all things **thelypthoric**. Consequently, he was blind from syphilis by the age of thirty." *(compare **unnun**)*

thrimmel /THRIM el/ v • To pay a debt in a mean and niggardly fashion.

Here it is: the perfect word for those people who just can't pay up gracefully. All the world hates a **thrimmeller**. And yet this species of tightfist prospers.

"As a mob enforcer with intellectual aspirations, Luther enjoyed peppering his shakedowns with five-dollar words. 'Listen, bub,' he would say while hanging a debtor out the window by his ankles, 'Quit yer **thrimmelling**, or yer sidewalk pizza, see?'" *(compare **swedge**)*

timeserver /TIME serv er/ n • A person who changes his opinions to fit the times, or to be compliant with a superior.

These spineless jellyfish are everywhere. Their only talent, a pernicious knack for self-preservation, is enough to ensure that they will never be eradicated completely.

"As a high-level bureaucrat and professional **timeserver**, Beisswenger had so attuned his sensitive antennae to the slightest shift in the political winds that he had managed to survive five different administrations. As for his official duties, no one could remember what they were."

*(compare **ecomaniac, fart-sucker**)*

tittery-whoppet /TIT *er ee* WOP *it*/ n • An archaic euphemism for the vagina.

Although this word is not exactly an insult, it is the most absurd euphemism for the female genitalia that the authors have found after many months of diligent searching. It is difficult to imagine how one could retain even a spark of ardor after saying or hearing this word during a romantic encounter. "Oh! Darling! That's it...touch my **tittery-whoppet!**"

On the flip side of the coin, the silliest term for the penis that the authors have yet seen is probably *Polyphemus*. Polyphemus was the original one-eyed monster, the cyclops that devoured several of Ulysses' men. Aside from being somewhat obtuse, this word is also quaintly hopeful. Doubtless there is an allusion from the classics denoting a crippled, half-blind midget that would be far more fitting than that of a mighty, towering, single-eyed monster, but we don't know what it is.

(*compare* **aerocolpos, licktwat**)

tomalley /*tuh* MOLL *ee*/ n • The green, slimy liver of a cooked lobster.

There are, incidentally, two types of people in the world: those who like **tomalley,** and those who don't especially care for ill-smelling, mucuslike substances harvested from the innards of animals.

"After Mrs. Pendergrast reiterated her pronouncement about the **tomalley** being the 'best part' of the lobster, little Joe insisted she take his in return for both claws."

tosspot /TOSS *pot*/ n • A drunkard.
[From the phrase *to toss a pot,* to drink a pot]

tosspot

What a charming and evocative little word **tosspot** is. Should it be updated to take into account the alcohol receptacles of today? *Tossbottle* has a nice ring to it.

"Hank, the neighborhood **tosspot,** could never seem to get his old pickup truck off blocks and running again. But he just loved to tinker, and much to the consternation of his neighbors he spent the better part of every weekend whaling away under the hood with a ball-peen hammer while abominably drunk."

(*compare* **barlichood, debacchate**)

tribade /*trib ADE*/ n • A woman, especially one with a large clitoris, who practices tribadism; a female genital rubber.

Tribade is a word with a long and worthy pedigree. In the first century A.D., the famed Roman poet Martial wrote: "Philaenis the **tribade** pedicates* boys, and stiffer than a man in one day work eleven girls."

(*compare* **fricatrice**)

tribadism /*TRIB ud ism*/ n • Genital rubbing between women. Also, any rubbing of the female genitalia that results in orgasm.

Tribadism comes from the Greek *tribas* (rubbing).

"Denise thanked heaven her parents had sent her to horseback riding camp as a little girl, or else she might never have stumbled upon the joys of **tribadism** when learning how to canter that fateful afternoon."

trichotillomania /*TRIK o til o MAY nee uh*/ n • The tearing out of one's own hair, as in certain disordered states of mind.

Everyday events that may drive one to **trichotillomania** include locking oneself out of one's car and leaving one's plane ticket on the dresser while one speeds to the airport.

"The **trichotillomania** first appeared not long after Prescott filled in his ticket wrong and missed the lottery jackpot by a single digit—it had never completely gone away since."

triorchid /*try OR kid*/ n • A man with three testicles. Also, figuratively, an extremely lascivious man.

"Born with 'one to spare,' Gustav, the alcoholic **triorchid,** enjoyed telling everyone within earshot exactly how it felt to be one of the horniest men alive."

(*compare* **polymasthus**)

---

*Pedicate: To debauch via the anus.

troat /TROAT/ v • To cry out like a rutting buck. n • The cry of a rutting buck.

The authors know of no better word for a bellowing mating call.

"Mortified, Winchester realized he had shattered the predawn silence—and awoken everyone in the lodge—by **troating** during the act of love." (*compare **fream***)

trocar /TRO *kar*/ n • A hollow tube farmers insert into the rectums of cattle to release trapped gas.

To be sure, **trocars**, which at first glance resemble hand-held drills, do have other uses, such as the draining of liquid from body cavities. But nothing quite as humorous as deflating steers.

"One of little Timmy's least favorite chores on the farm was buggering the stud bull with a **trocar** every afternoon."

troilism /TROY *lism*/ n • Sex between three partners; *ménage à trois*.

trocar

troilism

Troilism comes from the French *trois* (three). Which begs the question: why are the English words for so many sexual concepts (**frottage, renifleur, retifism**) so often French-derived? And where along the line did English speakers decide to attach the word "French" ("French toast," "French kiss," "French tickler") to anything that was either sexy or tasted good? Do the French, like blondes, have more fun, or do we just like to think that they do?

"Smitty was overjoyed that his wife had finally agreed to partake in **troilism** for his thirtieth birthday—until he saw that her choice of a third was the hairy plumber from downstairs." (*compare* **bivirist**)

trugabelly /TRUG *uh bell ee*/ n • A short and dirty fellow assigned to the most menial tasks.

This poor drudge is perhaps more an object of pity than scorn. On the other hand, who would not object to being called a **trugabelly**? Clearly this is not a *nice* word.

"Frustrated by her billionaire husband's lack of attention, the trophy wife had no recourse but to lavish all of her considerable affections upon the old **trugabelly** who manured the grounds on Tuesdays—the one with the gap-toothed smile." (*compare* **barkled**)

tumbrel /TUM *brel*/ n • 1) A cart that is used for transporting dung. 2) A person who is drunk to the point of vomiting.

While it can't hurt to know another way to refer to a dung cart, the second definition of this word is more germane. The next time an overly soused guest deposits his dinner on your bathroom floor, you will be able to refrain from issuing a hackneyed batch of expletives and instead correctly peg him with the proper terminology.

(*compare* **bespew**)

turdefy /TURD *if eye*/ v • To turn into feces.

[*turd* from Old English *tord* + *-fy* to make]

A point of usage: It is the authors' understanding that

twitchel

this verb can be both transitive and intransitive. That is, it can refer to the act of becoming shit as well as the act of turning something else into shit.

"After his new sous-chef **turdified** the rack of lamb—in addition to the black bean soup, the *crème brulée,* and even the *frisée* greens—Chef Claude snapped his fingers and two burly dishwashers whisked the unlucky lad into the walk-in freezer. The wily old veteran of the backbiting culinary wars was not born yesterday; interrogation quickly determined which of his competitors had sent the saboteur."

(*compare **alothen***)

twee /TWEE/ adj • Overly cute.

"Jessie tried very hard to get along with his dorm mate, a **twee** surfer boy who always wore pastels and was rather *too* fond of unicorns. Alas, it proved to be impossible, and the two of them spent the rest of the semester maintaining a sullen silence."

twitchel /TWICH ul/ n • A childish old man.

"Ever since his stroke last August, Mr. Dodwell had become more and more of a **twitchel**. What a tragedy it was to see the once-proud drill sergeant reduced to a squalling brat who would cry when he didn't get a sweetie after dinner."

· U ·

ucalegon /yoo KAL eh gon/ n • A neighbor whose house is on fire.

[From the name of a Trojan chieftan whose house was set ablaze by the Greeks]

Not a word to use every day, and not a particularly insulting one, either. But the authors still feel that **ucalegon** is interesting enough to warrant inclusion in the present volume. If life ever does offer an opportunity to use this word, you would be wise to seize it, as another chance may never come.

"Mingling with the crowd gathered outside the burning dwelling, the ill-starred lexicographer simply could not restrain himself; after smugly flaunting the word **ucalegon** several dozen times, he was set upon by his neighbors and cast into the flames." (*compare* **epicaricacy**)

unasinous /yoo NASS in us/ adj • Equally stupid.

[Latin *unus* one + *asinus* ass]

The reader may well wonder how to employ such a word, but **unasinous** is more useful than it first appears. For instance, in describing both sides of a foolish argument.

"Controlled experiments with the Chinese finger trap proved what the townsfolk had suspected all along: the Underhill twins were indeed **unasinous**."

unipygic /yoo ni PIE gik/ adj • Having but one ass cheek.

[Latin *unus* one + Greek *pyge* rump]

Literally, half-assed.

A good word for veiled insults:

"...And so I introduce to you, ladies and gentlemen, the man whose **unipygic** leadership has brought this company to where it is today...." (*compare* **apoglutic, kakopygian**)

unnun /un NUN/ v • To strip a nun of her position or character.

While the strict definition of this word doesn't specify that it involves engaging in sex with a nun, we are left to ask: How else would one strip a nun of her character—encourage her to gamble? And while the deviants reading this book will in all probability never have a chance to **unnun** a holy sister, now at least they can fantasize about it with the correct terminology.

"When Pablo's sweetheart joined the convent he refused to acknowledge defeat, but spent the rest of his days dreaming up futile schemes to **unnun** her."

(*compare* **thelypthoric**)

uranism /YOO run ism/ n • Homosexuality among "physically normal" men.

The authors' source does not specify exactly what is meant by "physically normal."

"Sutton's doctoral thesis, '**Uranism** in the Prison System: Past, Present, and Future' yielded him the benefit of a small degree of public acclaim—and a surfeit of phone numbers from strapping ex-convicts."

urinarium /YOO rin AIR ee um/ n • A tank that collects the runoff urine from a stable and stores it for future use.

unnun

Urine collected in this way could then be used for fertilizer, or perhaps even for **lant** or **lotium**.

"As punishment for breaking the eggs, the bossman ordered Oliver to swab out the farm's **urinarium** in the noon heat." *(compare **stercorary**)*

urinous /YOO *rin us*/ adj • Smelling like, marked by the presence of, or resembling urine.

A word as useful in the big city as it is on the farm.

"The slight **urinous** tinge to the soup was the tipoff that eventually led to the arrest of the vengeful caterer."

*(compare **fecaloid**)*

uriposiac /yoo *rip* O *zee ak*/ n • A drinker of urine.

[Greek *ouron* urine + *posis* drinking]

Yes, they do shoot horses, and some people do drink urine. Why? In certain circles it is held to be medically beneficial to drink your first batch of the day (Gandhi is reported to have quaffed a cup of his own special home brew every morning). Other folks like to imbibe someone else's; maybe they just like the taste.

"The ideological battle at the clinic was fast becoming an ugly one. Now the **uriposiac** camp of doctors attempted to take the upper hand by secretly spiking the patient's IV bags with their panacea. The results were not encouraging."

*(compare **leint**)*

urning /URN *ing*/ n • A homosexual.

An uncommon but fairly straightforward word for someone who isn't straight.

"Johnny Flowers, cabaret star extraordinaire, changed into yet another sequined outfit—his third for the evening—and regaled the sold-out crowd with his emotional torch song 'I've Got a Yearning for an **Urning**.'"

(*compare* **poger**)

urolagnia /YOO *ro* LAG *nee uh*/ n • Sexual excitement from urine or urination, either one's own or another's.

"Few fans enjoyed drinking quart after quart of warm beer at the ballpark as much as Troy, whose **urolagnia** also made the trip to the men's room every other inning a keenly-awaited treat."

urolagniac /YOO *ro* LAG *nee ak*/ n • A deviant who derives sexual pleasure from urine or urination, his own or another person's.

"Medcorp executives prayed to God that the press wouldn't catch wind of that little business concerning Fred, the **urolagniac** lab assistant, and his nocturnal bacchanals." (*compare* **renifleur**)

urticate /URT *ik ate*/ v • To flog with stinging nettles: a form of treatment for paralysis.

"Mr. Witherspoon enjoyed a good, stiff **urtication** in the morning, and whenever possible would follow it up by sacking one or two members of his staff."

(*compare* **mastigophoric**)

uxoravalent /*ooks or* AHV *uh lent*/ adj • Able to have sex only with one's wife.

It is unclear why we need a word for such a rare condition. There is no real explanation, other than the fact that lexicographers like to have all their bases covered.

(*compare* **uxorovalent**)

uxorious /ooks OR ee us/ adj • Overly fond of one's wife.

Uxorious describes the man who dotes on and idolizes his wife to sickening excess.

"His coworkers finally dropped a piano on Harlan, the **uxorious** moving man, when he said he was taking a third job so he could afford music lessons for his tone-deaf bride." (*compare **maritality***)

uxorovalent /ooks or O vuh lent/ adj • Able to have sex only with someone *other* than one's wife.

Oh, what a difference a letter makes.

(*compare **uxoravalent***)

uzzard /UZZ ard/ n • A third-generation bastard.

"Many were the nights that Stevens the **uzzard,** after consuming too much crème de menthe, would rise to his feet and loudly proclaim his pride in his heritage, or lack thereof. 'My father was a bastard,' he would declare slurringly, 'and his father before him was a bastard as well!'"

(*compare **adulterine, yaldson***)

vagient /*VAY jee ent*/ adj • Crying like a child.

"Sensing that his political life hung in the balance, the president went on national TV and made a **vagient** speech in which he admitted to every sin he had committed since the third grade."

vaginismus /*vaj in IZ mus*/ n • Spasmodic tightening of the muscles around the vagina, resulting from an extreme aversion to penetration.

"Zelda's date had a great sense of humor and beautiful eyes, but something about the way he ate the bratwurst triggered violent **vaginismus** in her."

(*compare* **colpoxerosis**)

valgus /*VAL gus*/ n • A bowlegged person.

"Tony, the pint-sized **valgus,** had all the physical tools of a champion goat jockey. All he lacked was the desire."

varietist /*ver EYE uh tist*/ n • A person with unorthodox appetites.

"The marriage that had started out so well was doomed to fail, for she was a **varietist,** and he more of a meat-and-potatoes kind of lover." (*compare* **paraphiliac**)

ventose /ven TOSE/ adj • Verbally flatulent; full of pomp, conceit, and bombast.

[Latin *ventus* wind]

"Because of the **ventose** talk show host's ability to fill endless hours of airtime with his inane rantings, the very same quality that had always caused most people to loathe him instantly was now making him a very rich man indeed." (*compare **blatherskite, cacafuego***)

verbigerator /ver BIG er ATE or/ n • One who senselessly repeats clichés.

"People considered him a sage, and his advice was eagerly sought by luminaries from far and wide. No one seemed to realize that Hanson was nothing more than a senile old **verbigerator** with a talent for continually firing off platitudes." (*compare **echolalia***)

vernalagnia /vern uh LAG nee uh/ n • Heightened sexual desire in the springtime.

In other words, spring fever. A disease with only one known cure...a long, cold shower. (*compare **nisus***)

vetanda /ve TAN duh/ n, pl • Things that should not be done.

There are so many things in life that should not be done, and so many people doing them. It seems odd that the word for this concept is not more widely known.

The parson thought he might enjoy
a harmless tryst with Ms. Lacroix.
But the memoranda
*of their **vetanda***
was a club-footed, half-wit boy.

viraginity

viraginity /vih ruh JIN it ee/ n • Manliness in a woman.

Viraginity has no etymological connection to "virginity," and although the adjectival form of this word is *viraginian*, there is nothing in the literature to indicate that the condition is not equally common in Arkansas or North Carolina.

Viraginity loosely describes the attributes of a *virago* (originally a strong female warrior, later a bold, impudent woman). All three words stem from the Latin *vir* (man).

"Lucy read the warning on the diet pills and figured she was safe: after all, how bad could '**viraginity**' be? As a result, her once-ample chest now resembled that of a slightly overweight ten-year-old boy."   (*compare* **gynander**)

vomiturition /VOM ich yoor ISH un/ n • Vomiting with violent spasms but little brought up. Also, repeated unproductive vomiting.

"When his attorney told him just how much the divorce was going to cost him, Mr. Pecksniff fell victim to a prolonged bout of **vomiturition**."   (*compare* **keck**)

wamble /*WOM bul*/ v • To heave and roll, as an upset stomach; also, to rumble in the stomach, as hard-to-digest food.

"Three hot dogs and two ice creams later, and my poor stomach was **wambling** as it had never **wambled** before."

(*compare* **collywobbles**)

wetewold /*WAIT wald*/ n • A patient cuckold.

[Middle English *cokewold* cuckold, with substitution of *wete* wit, to know]

"Tyson the **wetewold** knew that his wife was making time with most of his buddies, but he didn't care. As long as her extracurricular activities freed him up to play with his beloved electric trains, he was content."

(*compare* **wittol**)

windbroach /*WIND broach*/ n • An inferior fiddler.

Life is long, and one never knows when a necessity might arise to insult a lousy violinist—perhaps at the next fourth-grade talent show you attend. Be prepared: keep **windbroach** at the ready. (*compare* **cantabank**)

witling /*WIT ling*/ n • A person who lacks understanding or intelligence.

"Günter, the leader of the dangerous expedition to the

high Andes, was an imposing man with an air of imperturbable confidence about him; unfortunately—as everyone was about to discover—he was also a world-class **witling**."

(*compare **mumchance***)

wittol /*WIT all*/ n • A contented cuckold; a man unbothered by his wife's infidelity.

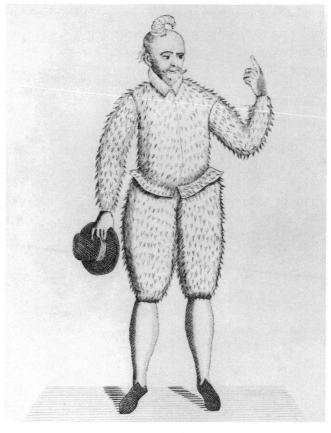

wittol

"Gregor the **wittol** breathed a sigh of relief. The months of tension in bed, the tedious arguments every night, the awkward and unsatisfying sex—all these were things of the past, now that the virile Fernando had moved in next door." (*compare **wetewold***)

woodpusher /*WOOD push er*/ n • A poor chess player.

"Determined that their son would be the next Kasparov, the Sigorskis refused to recognize that he was a **woodpusher** with more interest in dolls than in a chess board. Their insistence that he play the game sent him to the sanitarium before he was eleven."

· X ·

xanthodont /*ZAN thoh dont*/ adj • Having yellow teeth.

A distinguishing characteristic of smokers and coffee drinkers.

"Baking soda, rinses, bleach: none of it worked. Only the airbrush could help Natalie, the **xanthodont** fashion model."

xysma /*ZIZE muh*/ n • "Material, like bits of membrane, found in the stools of diarrhea," according to *Webster's Universal Unabridged Dictionary* of 1936. (We thought it best not to tinker with this one.)

However could this charming word have fallen into disuse? It is definitely one of the most revolting entries in any dictionary—and you had to make it all the way to the Xs for it. Think of it as a little reward for getting this far.

(*compare* **lientery**)

· Y ·

yaldson /*YALD son*/ n • The son of a prostitute.

"Preston's upbringing in the bordello had been a happy one. He was lavished with attention from the girls, who lovingly called him 'Peaches' and would often braid flowers in his hair. It wasn't until his first day at the academy, when he heard the word **yaldson** uttered with scorn, that he felt a twinge of shame." (*compare **uzzard***)

yeevil /*YEE vil*/ n • A dung fork.

"The Richardsons set a most impressive table: china aplenty, serving plates and soup bowls abounding, and every conceivable type of utensil for each one of the innumerable courses they typically served during a formal meal. Given the miserable quality of the food itself, however, they might as well have given each guest a **yeevil** and left it at that."

· Z ·

zoilus /ZOY *lus*/ n • An envious person.

[From *Zoilus,* the name of a Greek famed for his criticisms of Homer]

"Andrew was cursed with a jealous and scheming faculty advisor, who ridiculed and belittled him so mercilessly that he ended up abandoning his Ph.D to take a job teaching remedial education in a small rural high school. Several months later, the **zoilus** published the work under his own name." (*compare* **mome**)

zooerastia /*zoo er ASS tee uh*/ n • The practice of engaging in sexual activity with an animal.

"Father Rick could never remember whether **zooerastia** was a mortal sin or a venial one, so he told the man in the confessional to say twenty Hail Marys and made a mental note to pray for the man's soul."

zowerswopped /ZOW *er swopt*/ adj • Foul-tempered.
If we've given cause to offend,
rest assured we'd never intend
to make you feel bad,
unpleasant, or sad,
with this **zowerswopped** *book that we've penned.*

A Select Bibliography

The American Heritage Dictionary of the English Language. Boston: Houghton Mifflin Company, 1980.

The American Illustrated Medical Dictionary. 9th ed. Philadelphia and London: W.B. Saunders Company, 1918.

Bailey, Nathaniel. *An Universal Etymological English Dictionary.* 18th ed. London, 1761.

Black, Donald Chain. *Spoonerisms, Sycophants, and Sops.* New York: Harper and Row, 1988.

Black's Law Dictionary. 4th ed. St. Paul, Minn.: West Publishing Company, 1951.

Black's Medical Dictionary. 35th ed. Totowa, N.J.: Barnes & Noble Books, 1987.

Blake, Roger. *The American Dictionary of Sexual Terms.* Hollywood, Calif.: Century Publishing Co., 1964.

Bowler, Peter. *The Superior Person's Book of Words.* New York: Dell Laurel, 1982.

———. *The Superior Person's Second Book of Weird and Wondrous Words.* Boston: David R. Godine, 1992.

Brent, Irwin M., and Rod L. Evans. *More Weird Words.* New York: Berkley Books, 1995.

Byrne, Josefa Heifitz. *Mrs. Byrne's Dictionary of Unusual, Obscure, and Preposterous Words.* New York: Citadel Press and University Books, 1974.

The Century Dictionary and Cyclopedia. New York: Century Company, 1889–1914.

Chambers, Ephraim. *Cyclopedia: Or, An Universal Dictionary of Arts and Sciences.* London: 1791.

Cockeram, Henry. *The English Dictionarie of 1623.* New York: Huntington Press, 1930.

The Compact Oxford English Dictionary. 2d ed. Oxford: Oxford University Press, 1991.

Davies, T. Lewis. *A Supplementary Glossary*. London: George Bell and Sons, 1881.

Dickson, Paul. *Words*. New York: Delacorte Press, 1982.

Dictionary of Psychology. 3d British Commonwealth ed. London: Peter Owen, 1972.

Dunglison, Robley. *A Dictionary of Medical Science*. Philadelphia: Henry C. Lea, 1874.

Dunkling, Leslie. *The Guiness Book of Curious Words*. Enfield, Middlesex: Guiness Publishing Ltd., 1994.

Ehrlich, Eugene. *The Highly Selective Dictionary for the Extraordinarily Literate*. New York: HarperCollins Publishers, 1997.

———. *The Highly Selective Thesaurus for the Extraordinary Literate*. New York: HarperCollins Publishers, 1994.

Elster, Charles Harrington. *There's a Word for It! A Grandiloquent Guide to Life*. New York: Pocket Books, 1996.

Funk & Wagnall's New Standard Dictionary of the English Language. Medallion edition. New York: Funk & Wagnall's Company, 1942.

Goldenson, Robert, and Kenneth Anderson. *The Wordsworth Dictionary of Sex*. Hertfordshire: Wordsworth Editions Ltd., 1994.

Gordon, Dale. *The Dominion Sex Dictionary*. 1967.

Gould, George M. *An Illustrated Dictionary of Medicine, Biology, and Allied Sciences*. 4th ed. Philadelphia: P. Blakiston, Son & Co., 1898.

Grambs, David. *Dimboxes, Epopts, and Other Quidams*. New York: Workman Publishing, 1986.

———. *The Endangered English Dictionary*. New York: W.W. Norton & Company, 1994.

Grose, Francis. *1811 Dictionary of the Vulgar Tongue*. London: Bibliophile Books, 1984.

———. *A Provincial Glossary; With a Collection of Local Proverbs, and Popular Superstitions*. 2d ed. London: S. Hooper, 1790.

Halliwell, James Orchard. *Dictionary of Archaic Words*. London: Bracken Books, 1989.

Hellweg, Paul. *The Insomniac's Dictionary*. New York: Ballantine Books, 1986.

Hinsie, Leland E. and Robert Campbell. *Psychiatric Dictionary*. New York: Oxford University Press, 1960.

Hook, J.N. *The Grand Panjandrum*. New York: Macmillan Publishing Company, 1980.

Hughes, Geoffrey. *Words in Time: A Social History of the English Vocabulary*. New York: Basil Blackwell Inc., 1988.

———. *Swearing: A Social History of Foul Language, Oaths and Profanity in English*. London: Penguin Books, 1991.

Johnson, Samuel. *A Dictionary of the English Language*. London: William Bell, 1783.

Kacirk, Jeffrey. *Forgotten English*. New York: William Morrow & Company, 1997.

Lempriere, J. *Lempriere's Classical Dictionary*. London: Milner and Company, 1887.

Love, Brenda. *Encyclopedia of Unusual Sex Practices*. New York: Barricade Books Inc., 1992.

Mackay, Charles. *Lost Beauties of the English Language*. London: Bibliophile Books, 1987.

The Merck Manual of Diagnosis and Therapy. 15th ed. Rahway, N.J.: Merck & Co., 1987.

Nare, Robert. *Nare's Glossary*. Charles Loeffler, 1825.

Partridge, Eric. *A Dictionary of Slang and Unconventional English*. New York: Macmillan Publishing Company, 1961.

———. *Origins: A Short Etymological Dictionary of Modern English*. New York: Macmillan Publishing Company, 1958.

Perry, William. *The Royal Standard English Dictionary*. Brookfield, Mass.: E. Merriam & Co., 1806.

Psychiatric Dictionary. 3d ed. New York: Oxford University Press, 1960.

Q.P.B. Dictionary of Difficult Words. New York: Quality Paperback Book Club, 1994.

Ray, J. *A Collection of English Words Not Generally Used*. 4th ed. London: W. Otridge, 1768.

Rheingold, Howard. *They Have a Word for It*. Los Angeles: Jeremy P. Tarcher, 1988.

Richardson, Charles. *A New Dictionary of the English Language*. London: William Pickering, 1844.

Rocke, Russell. *The Grandiloquent Dictionary*. Englewood Cliffs, N.J.: Prentice-Hall Inc., 1972.

Rodale, Jerome Irving. *The Synonym Finder*. Emmaus, Pa.: Rodale Press, 1978.

Saussy, George Stone III. *The Logodaedalian's Dictionary of Interesting and Unusual Words*. Columbia, South Carolina: University of South Carolina Press, 1989.

Schmidt, J.E. *The Lecher's Lexicon*. New York: Bell Publishing Company, 1967.

Schur, Norman W. *1000 Most Obscure Words*. New York: Facts on File, 1990.

Sharman, Julian. *A Cursory History of Swearing*. New York: Burt Franklin, 1968.

Shipley, Joseph T. *Dictionary of Early English*. Paterson, N.J.: Littlefield, Adams, and Company, 1963.

The Signet/Mosby Medical Encyclopedia. New York: Penguin Books, 1987.

Sperling, Susan Kelz. *Lost Words of Love*. New York: Clarkson Potter Publishers, 1993.

Taber's Cyclopedic Medical Dictionary. 15th ed. Philadelphia: F. A. Davis Company, 1985.

Trench, Richard C. *Dictionary of Obsolete English*. New York: Philosophical Library, 1958.

Universal Dictionary of the English Language. New York: Peter Fenelon Collier, 1898.

Walker, John. *Critical Pronouncing Dictionary and Expositor of the English Language*. New York: Collins and Hannay, 1831.

Warrack, Alexander. *The Concise Scots Dictionary*. Poole Dorset: New Orchard Editions, 1988.

Webster, Noah, *An American Dictionary of the English Language*. Springfield. Mass.: George and Charles Merriam, 1857.

Webster's New International Dictionary. 2d ed. Merriam-Webster, 1936.

Webster's Third New International Dictionary. Springfield, Mass.: G. & C. Merriam Company, 1961.

Willy, Vander, and Fisher. *The Illustrated Encyclopedia of Sex*. New York: Cadillac Publishing Company, 1950.

Worchester, Joseph. *A Dictionary of the English Language*. Boston: Samuel Walker & Co., 1873.

Wright, Joseph. *The English Dialect Dictionary*. London: Henry Frowde, 1898.

Wright, Thomas. *Dictionary of Obsolete and Provincial English*. London: Henry G. Bohn, 1857.

Zettler, Howard G. *-Ologies and -Isms*. Detroit, Mich.: Gale Research Company, 1978.